This book was brought
to you by the
Naumes Family Foundation

At Issue

| Alcohol Abuse

Other Books in the At Issue Series:

At Issue

Alcohol Abuse

Christine Watkins, Book Editor

GREENHAVEN PRESS
A part of Gale, Cengage Learning

GALE
CENGAGE Learning·

Detroit • New York • San Francisco • New Haven, Conn • Waterville, Maine • London

Elizabeth Des Chenes, *Managing Editor*

© 2012 Greenhaven Press, a part of Gale, Cengage Learning

Gale and Greenhaven Press are registered trademarks used herein under license.

For more information, contact:
Greenhaven Press
27500 Drake Rd.
Farmington Hills, MI 48331-3535
Or you can visit our Internet site at gale.cengage.com

For product information and technology assistance, contact us at

Gale Customer Support, 1-800-877-4253
For permission to use material from this text or product, submit all requests online at
www.cengage.com/permissions

Further permissions questions can be emailed to permissionrequest@cengage.com

Articles in Greenhaven Press anthologies are often edited for length to meet page requirements. In addition, original titles of these works are changed to clearly present the main thesis and to explicitly indicate the author's opinion. Every effort is made to ensure that Greenhaven Press accurately reflects the original intent of the authors. Every effort has been made to trace the owners of copyrighted material.

Cover image copyright © Images.com/Corbis.

LIBRARY OF CONGRESS CATALOGING-IN-PUBLICATION DATA

Alcohol abuse / Christine Watkins, book editor.
    p. cm. -- (At issue)
    Includes bibliographical references and index.
    ISBN 978-0-7377-5542-8 (hardback) -- ISBN 978-0-7377-5543-5 (paperback)
    1. Alcoholism--United States. 2. Alcoholism. 3. Youth--Alcohol use--United
States. 4. Drinking of alcoholic beverages. I. Watkins, Christine, 1951-
    HV5292.A372 2012
    362.2920973--dc23

                                                                    2011037006

Printed in the United States of America
1 2 3 4 5 6 7 16 15 14 13 12

Contents

Introduction

In November 2007 seventeen-year-old Ryan Bourque left a party hosted by his friend's parents at their home in Lawrence, Massachusetts, and was killed in a car accident while driving drunk. In December 2007 a passerby found the lifeless body of sixteen-year-old Julia Gonzalez in a park in Turlock, California. The toxicology report later revealed Julia had died of acute alcohol poisoning. Her blood-alcohol content at the time of her death was more than six times the legal limit for adult intoxication in California, which would be equivalent to having sixteen drinks in one hour. In October 2008 seventeen-year-old Taylor Meyer stumbled into a Norfolk, Virginia, swamp after a night of binge drinking at the home of one of her friends. She was found drowned later that night. And in December 2008 Poway, California high school cheerleader Veronica Aguirre was at a party when she texted her girlfriend, "I'm hammered." While driving home shortly after sending the message, Veronica lost control of her car, which then rolled over several times, and was killed instantly. All of these incidents involved underage drinking parties. And because of what are known as "social host liability laws," the hosts of these parties could be held responsible for the deaths and subject to criminal prosecution.

Social host liability laws hold the host legally responsible for what happens to intoxicated guests as well as for any damage the guests do to others. Such laws vary from state to state, but most focus on adults who allow liquor to be served to underage youth. In addition to having to pay for medical bills, property damage, and emotional pain and suffering, parents who break these social host laws are increasingly being sent to jail. In one Pennsylvania case, a parent was given a sentence of one to four-and-a-half years in prison for involuntary manslaughter after three teens died in a drunk-driving accident following a party the parent hosted. Furthermore, parents may be held accountable even if they are not home during the party or not aware that minors are drinking alcohol on the premises.

Most parents who host parties for their underage children have good intentions at heart, thinking they can control the situation and provide a safe environment. Many believe alcohol has become a customary part of American teenage culture and if teens are unable to party at parentally supervised homes, they will drink in cars, at parks, beaches, or other public places. For these reasons, Marsha Rosenbaum, a medical sociologist and founder of the *Safety First* project at The Drug Policy Alliance (DPA), is against the laws that penalize parents for hosting such parties. In the June 17, 2010, *New York Times* article "Room for Debate: Should Parents Be Jailed When Kids Drink?" Rosenbaum stated, "Arresting parents for trying to keep their teenagers safe is not the answer, and may ultimately do more harm than good." She worries that "targeting otherwise law-abiding, responsible parents may actually reduce teen safety." While emphasizing that adults need to be extremely vigilant when hosting teenage parties, Massachusetts trial lawyer Robert M. Delahunt Jr. agrees with Rosenbaum in some respects and fears that social host laws can punish innocent, well-meaning parents. Delahunt explained to Don Aucoin for the August 28, 2010, *Boston Globe* article "Are You Responsible?" that adolescents can be quite cunning in bypassing house party rules. "You could be at one end of the house, the kids are in the basement, you think they're watching a movie, somebody brings a water bottle with a large amount of vodka, and you've 'allowed' it. There are genuine instances where parents just don't know because the kids have thwarted them."

Many other parents and experts, however, adamantly oppose underage drinking parties and advocate in favor of strong social host liability laws. They would like to see penalties ratcheted up significantly and contend that more public-awareness campaigns—like "Adults Who Host Lose the Most"—are needed to educate people about the dangers of underage drinking. They assert that there is no safe environment for someone under the age of twenty-one to drink alcohol. David S. Anderson, professor of education and human development at George Mason University in Virginia agrees. In the 2010 *New York Times* article, "Room for Debate: Should Parents Be Jailed When Kids Drink?" Anderson stated, "Social host laws are needed to communicate clearly that underage drinking is not acceptable. While a parent may have the intention of limiting a teenager's (and his or her friends') exposure to drunk driving by hosting a party, exposing teenagers to alcohol even in that setting can result in harm, like alcohol poisoning, sexual abuse, violence, drunk driving, and more." Anderson also insists that a comprehensive approach is necessary to combat the problem of underage drinking, an approach that should include prevention and early intervention. In addition to laws and policies, "we also need to find out why adolescents drink and then address the underlying reasons for their decisions about alcohol use or non-use."

Indeed, alcohol abuse among adolescents is a serious problem. Medical research continues to expose dangerous health consequences, including such developmental brain damage as memory impairment and an inability to focus. Furthermore, studies have shown that young people who start drinking before age fifteen are five times more likely to develop alcohol problems later in life. The authors of the viewpoints in *At Issue: Alcohol Abuse* discuss other risks and possible solutions surrounding the problem of alcohol abuse as it affects people of all ages.

1

Excessive Alcohol Consumption Creates Numerous Health and Safety Risks

Research Society on Alcoholism

The Research Society on Alcoholism (RSA) provides a forum for communication among researchers who share common interests in alcoholism. The Society's purpose is to promote research that can lead the way toward prevention and treatment of alcoholism.

Essentially every American is affected by alcoholism in some way, whether directly through the alcohol abuse of a family member or indirectly through the impact of alcoholism on society, which costs the United States approximately $400 billion annually. Heavy drinking—which can be defined as having five or more drinks in a single day at least once a week for males, and four or more for females—has been linked to heart disease, stroke, numerous cancers, and fetal alcohol syndrome, as well as to automobile accidents and domestic violence. There are some encouraging developments in the treatment of alcoholism, however. Scientists and genetic researchers are learning more about its cause and development and, as a result, are creating more effective medications and treatment programs to reduce abusive drinking.

Research Society on Alcoholism, *Impact of Alcoholism and Alcohol Induced Disease on America*, RSA White Paper, April 20, 2011, pp. 1–5. Reproduced by permission.

Alcoholism is a serious disease that affects the lives of millions of Americans, devastates families, compromises national preparedness, depresses economic vitality, and burdens the country's health care systems. This disease touches virtually all Americans. More than half of all adults have a family history of alcoholism or problem drinking. Three in ten adults 18 years of age and over have had alcoholism and/or engaged in alcohol abuse at some point in their lives and their drinking will impact their families, communities, and society as a whole. Untreated addiction costs America $400 billion annually and recent research indicates that alcoholism and alcohol abuse alone cost the nation's economy approximately $185 billion each year. Fifteen percent of this amount is the cost of medical consequences and alcohol treatment; more than 70 percent is due to reduced, lost and forgone earnings; and the remainder is the cost of lost workforce productivity, accidents, violence, and premature death.

The Centers for Disease Control and Prevention (CDC) ranks alcohol as the third leading cause of preventable death in the United States.

This paper documents the deleterious impact of heavy drinking, alcohol abuse and alcoholism on the United States. As explained more fully below, heavy drinking (defined as having five or more drinks in a single day at least once a week for males, and 4 or more for females), contributes to illness in each of the top three causes of death: heart disease, cancer, and stroke. The Centers for Disease Control and Prevention (CDC) ranks alcohol as the third leading cause of preventable death in the United States. According to the National Institute on Alcohol Abuse and Alcoholism (NIAAA), 3 in 10 U.S. adults engage in at-risk drinking patterns and thus would benefit from counseling or a referral for further evaluation.

The CDC also links excessive alcohol use, such as heavy drinking and binge drinking, to numerous immediate health risks that pose a menace not only to those consuming alcohol, but also to those around them including traffic fatalities, unintentional firearm injuries, domestic violence and child maltreatment, risky sexual behaviors, sexual assault, miscarriage and stillbirth, and a combination of physical and mental birth defects that last a lifetime.

Alcohol's Role in Hypertension, Heart Disease, and Cancer

People who drink alcohol excessively have a one and a half to two times increased frequency of high blood pressure. The association between alcohol and high blood pressure is particularly clear when alcohol intake exceeds 5 drinks per day, and the prevalence of hypertension is doubled at 6 or more drinks per day. Among the risk factors for hypertension that have the potential to be modified, alcohol is second only to obesity in its observed contribution to the prevalence of hypertension in men. These findings have yet to be verified in women. When managing hypertensive patients, however, relevant counseling can bring about a reduction in high blood pressure.

Numerous studies suggest that moderate alcohol consumption (no more than 2 drinks/day for men and 1 drink/day for women) helps protect against heart disease by raising HDL (good) cholesterol and reducing plaque accumulations in the arteries. Alcohol also has a mild anticoagulating effect, keeping platelets from clumping together to form clots. Both actions can reduce the risk of heart attack but exactly how alcohol influences either one still remains unclear. On the other hand, consumption of more than three drinks a day has a direct toxic effect on the heart. Heavy drinking, particularly over time, can damage the heart and lead to high blood pressure, alcoholic cardiomyopathy, congestive heart failure, and hemorrhagic stroke. Heavy drinking also impairs fat metabolism and raises triglyceride levels.

According to the NIAAA, considerable evidence suggests a connection between heavy alcohol consumption and increased risk for cancer, with an estimated 2 to 4 percent of all cancer cases thought to be caused either directly or indirectly by alcohol. A strong association exists between alcohol use and cancers of the esophagus, pharynx, and mouth, whereas a more controversial association links alcohol with breast cancer. Together, these cancers killed an estimated 58,970 people in the United States in 2010.

Alcohol's effects on the developing brain are life-long.

Alcohol's Effects During Prenatal Development

Data from the CDC indicate that 12 percent of pregnant women drink alcohol. Approximately one in 100 babies is born with one of the Fetal Alcohol Spectrum Disorders (FASD). Alcohol's effects on the developing brain are life-long and impact many behaviors including motor and sensory skills, social skills, and learning abilities. As individuals with FASD grow up, they are at greater risk for a variety of secondary disabilities including other psychiatric problems, illicit drug use, delinquent or criminal behavior, precocious or risky sexual activity, and academic failure. There is no known stage of pregnancy or quantity of alcohol consumption that is safe during pregnancy. Current research on the effects of early alcohol exposure includes not only prevention but also early life interventions, establishing and implementing more effective diagnostic tools, and understanding the mechanisms underlying the tragic outcomes associated with FASD.

Alcohol's Influence on Accidents and Violence

Alcohol plays a significant role in trauma by increasing both the likelihood and severity of injury. Heavy drinkers or alcohol abusers are more likely than others to be involved in a trauma event. Given similar circumstances, a drinker is also likely to be hurt more seriously than a non-drinker. Moreover, an estimated 27 percent of all trauma patients treated in emergency departments and hospitals are candidates for a brief alcohol intervention.

Alcohol exposure can also alter inflammatory responses and immune function and this can be exacerbated if there is an existing or concurrent injury. Research suggests that chronic heavy drinking depresses estrogen levels, nullifying estrogen's beneficial effects on the immune system and weakening a woman's ability to fight infections and tumors. Additionally, some research suggests that this detrimental effect may be compounded by an alcohol-induced elevation in steroidal hormones, known as glucocorticoids, which suppress immune responses in both men and women.

The relationship between alcohol or other substance abuse and domestic violence is complicated. Frequently either the perpetrator, the victim or both have been using alcohol heavily. According to the National Woman Abuse Prevention Project, some abusers rely on substance use (and abuse) as an excuse for becoming violent. Alcohol allows the abuser to "justify" abusive behavior. While an abuser's use of alcohol may have an effect on the severity of the abuse or the ease with which the abuser can justify their actions, an abuser does not become violent "because" drinking causes them to lose control of their temper.

According to the National Incident-Based Reporting System (NIBRS), nearly 11 percent of violent incidents reported in 2007 involved alcohol. In 2008, among victims who provided information about the offender's use of alcohol, about

36 percent perceived the offender to be under the influence of alcohol, which is a decrease from 44 percent in 1997. From 2004–2008, 19 percent of all alcohol-related violence was perpetrated by intimate partners, compared to 15 percent of violence in which alcohol was not involved. By contrast, an estimated 46 percent of stranger victimizations where the victim could determine the absence or presence of alcohol was perceived to be alcohol-related.

In 2008, 11,773 people were killed in alcohol-impaired-driving crashes. These alcohol-impaired-driving fatalities accounted for 32 percent of the total motor vehicle traffic fatalities in the United States and represented an average of one alcohol-impaired-driving fatality every 45 minutes. Traffic fatalities in alcohol-impaired-driving crashes fell by nearly 10 percent, from 13,041 in 2007 to 11,773 in 2008. Drivers are considered to be alcohol-impaired when their blood alcohol concentration (BAC) is .08 grams per deciliter (g/dL) or higher.

Over 1.4 million drivers were arrested for driving under the influence of alcohol or narcotics in 2008. This represents less than one percent of the 159 million self-reported episodes of alcohol-impaired driving in the U.S. each year. Of the 1,347 children age 14 and younger were killed in motor vehicle crashes in the U.S. in 2008, 216 (16 percent) of these fatalities occurred in alcohol-impaired driving crashes. Children riding in vehicles with drivers who had a BAC level of .08 or higher accounted for nearly half (99) of these deaths.

Alcohol's Effects on Young People and Military Personnel

According to the Substance Abuse & Mental Health Services Administration (SAMHSA), there were approximately 200,000 emergency room visits in 2009 by people under the age of 21 for injuries and other conditions linked to alcohol. This is compared to an estimated 40,000 annual emergency room visits linked to non-alcohol illicit substances by persons under 21.

The 2009 Youth Risk Behavior Survey found that among high school students surveyed, 9.7 percent reported driving after drinking alcohol one or more times during the 30 days before the survey. Another 28 percent indicated that they rode with a driver who had been drinking one or more times during the past 30 days.

Substance abuse is particularly problematic in younger adolescents because it is the time when individuals are most vulnerable to addiction.

The NIAAA, along with the National Institute on Drug Abuse (NIDA), and SAMHSA, have conducted research that demonstrates that substance abuse is particularly problematic in younger adolescents because it is the time when individuals are most vulnerable to addiction. According to the CDC, people aged 12 to 20 years drink almost 11 percent of all alcohol consumed in the United States, and 19 percent in this age category reported binge drinking. The NIAAA's *National Epidemiologic Survey on Alcohol-Related Conditions* (NESARC) found that 18 million Americans (8.5 percent of the population age 18 and older) suffer from alcohol use disorders (AUD), and only 7.1 percent of these individuals have received any treatment for their AUD in the past year.

NIAAA's NESARC survey sampled across the adult lifespan to allow researchers to identify how the emergence and progression of drinking behavior are influenced by changes in biology, psychology, and exposure to social and environmental inputs over a person's lifetime. Scientists at NIH [National Institutes of Health] are supporting research to promulgate preemptive care for fetuses, early childhood, and adolescents because children who engage in early alcohol use also typically display a wide range of adverse behavioral outcomes such as teenage pregnancy, delinquency, other substance use problems, and poor school achievement.

The prevalence of heavy drinking is higher in the military population (16.1 percent) than in a similar age and gender civilian population (12.9 percent). About one in four Marines (25.4 percent) and Army soldiers (24.5 percent) engages in heavy drinking; such a high prevalence of heavy alcohol use may be cause for concern about military readiness. Furthermore, the Army showed an increasing pattern of heavy drinking from 2002 to 2005. According to the Department of Defense's (DoD) *2005 Survey of Health Related Behaviors among Active Duty Military Personnel*, these patterns of alcohol abuse, which are often acquired in the military, frequently persist after discharge and are associated with the high rate of alcohol-related health disorders in the veteran population.

Individuals with alcoholism are also five times more likely to file workmen's compensation claims and they are more likely to cause injuries to themselves or others while on the job.

Alcohol's Influence on Economic Productivity

Employee alcohol use causes a variety of problems. It reduces productivity, impairs job performance, increases health care costs and can threaten public safety. Because 85 percent of heavy drinkers work, employers who aggressively address this problem can improve their employees' health while improving company performance. The federal government estimates that 8.9 percent of full-time workers (12.7 million people) have drinking problems. Alcohol costs American business an estimated $134 billion in productivity losses, mostly due to missed work; 65.3 percent of this cost was caused by alcohol-related illness, 27.2 percent due to premature death, and 7.5 percent to crime. People with alcoholism use twice as much sick leave as other employees. Individuals with alcoholism are also five times more likely to file workmen's compensation claims and they are more likely to cause injuries to themselves or others while on the job.

About 80 percent of people with alcohol problems work, yet fewer than 25 percent of those who need treatment get it. Untreated alcohol problems cost employers in several ways— greater health care expenses for injuries and illnesses, higher absenteeism, lower productivity, and more workers' compensation and disability claims. Research has shown that alcoholism treatment that is tailored to an individual's needs could be cost-effective for employers. Treatment substantially reduces drinking among people with alcoholism, and 40 to 60 percent of those treated for addiction remain abstinent after a year. By providing comprehensive health benefits that cover treatment for alcohol use disorders, employers can reduce their health care and personnel costs as well as contribute to employees' well-being and productivity.

While the high rates of use and abuse of alcohol are devastating problems of national importance, the good news is that this nation is poised to capitalize on unprecedented opportunities in alcohol research and prevention. These opportunities must be seized. Scientists are exploring new and exciting ways to prevent alcohol-associated accidents and violence and more prevention trials are developing methods to address problem alcohol use. Medications development is proceeding faster than anytime in the past 50 years, with many new compounds being developed and tested. Furthermore, researchers have identified discrete regions of the human genome that contribute to the inheritance of alcoholism. Improved genetic research will accelerate the rational design of medications to treat alcoholism and also improve understanding of the interaction and importance of heredity and environment in the development of alcoholism.

2

Moderate Alcohol Consumption Provides Health Benefits

U.C. Berkeley Wellness Letter

Founded in 1984, the U.C. Berkeley Wellness Letter relies on the expertise of the School of Public Health and other researchers at the University of California, Berkeley, as well as other top scientists from around the world to review the latest research on health and wellness issues.

A study funded by the National Institutes of Health found that drinking a moderate amount of alcohol every day is beneficial to health. For example, drinking alcohol helps prevent the formation of blood clots that cause heart attacks, and also raises blood levels of the good type of cholesterol (HDL), which help prevent hardening of the arteries. Furthermore, it appears that any alcoholic beverage—not just wine—in moderate amounts is protective. On the other hand, excessive amounts of alcohol can create serious health risks, such as liver damage and certain types of cancer; therefore, moderation is key for obtaining any health benefits from alcohol.

A recent, widely publicized study in the *New England Journal of Medicine* has led a lot of drinkers to congratulate themselves, and a lot of nondrinkers to wonder if they should start. "Drinking is good for your heart," the newspaper headlines announced, "and the more you drink, the better."

U.C. Berkeley Wellness Letter, "Should You Drink Alcohol for Your Heart?," www.berkeley wellness.com, August 2003, pp. 4–5. Reproduced by permission.

This was a well-designed study funded by the National Institutes of Health. It tracked the drinking habits of 38,000 men—all healthy at the beginning of the study—over 12 years. Men who drank at least three or four days a week had fewer heart attacks than those who drank less. It didn't matter what they drank—beer, wine, or spirits—or whether they drank it with meals. The positive news didn't end there. From the point of view of preventing heart attacks, drinking every day was better than drinking occasionally, and three drinks were better than one. Should you say hooray and head for the liquor store? We don't think so. Whether, when, and how much you should drink is a complex question, and the answer should be based on your current state of health, medical history, family history, age, sex, and other factors. If ever there was a double-edged sword, it's alcohol. It benefits people (and society) in some ways and devastates them in others. It is associated with some 100,000 deaths a year from disease and injury—more than the number of deaths from heart disease (estimated at perhaps 80,000) that it may prevent. And alcohol-related deaths occur mostly among the young.

Dozens of studies have found that moderate or light drinkers have a lower risk of heart disease.

Before you embrace alcohol as heart medicine, here are some Q & A's to consider.

Does Alcohol Protect the Heart?
If So, How?

Dozens of studies have found that moderate or light drinkers have a lower risk of heart disease—30 to 50% lower—than nondrinkers. There is hardly any argument about this now. Furthermore, researchers have found that even when moderate drinkers do have a heart attack, they have a lower risk of dying than teetotalers or heavy drinkers, and older people who drink moderately have a lower risk of heart failure. Alcohol raises blood levels of HDL ("good") cholesterol—which removes cholesterol from the bloodstream—and thus helps prevent hardening of the arteries (atherosclerosis). Alcohol also reduces the stickiness of platelets in the blood and thus helps prevent the blood clots that cause heart attacks. Consequently, some people compare alcohol to aspirin as a way to prevent clot formation or break up clots. And, yes, both can be helpful, if taken in small doses. But unlike aspirin, alcohol is intoxicating and potentially addictive. The point is that alcohol is only one of several things that may protect your heart. You can reduce your risk of heart disease without drinking at all.

How Clear Is the Evidence About the Protective Effect?

The evidence so far is very clear. Yet there has never been a large-scale, long-term, well-designed clinical trial testing the effect of alcohol. No matter how carefully conducted, nearly all the studies, including the one mentioned in the first paragraph, have been observational. That is, they followed groups of drinkers and nondrinkers and compared their health over time—a valuable kind of research, but never definitive. Remember, when the evidence about hormone replacement therapy (HRT) and its benefits for women's hearts—evidence gleaned from observational studies—was tested in controlled clinical trials, the benefits vanished. Indeed, HRT turned out to do some harm.

Moderate drinking may cut the risk of developing dementia, including Alzheimer's disease.

It is hard to separate alcohol from all the other factors that affect heart disease risk (that is, "control" for those factors) in a study. For instance, moderate drinkers may have healthier habits to begin with—and thus be less likely to have heart disease. Similarly, women taking HRT tended to lead healthier lives and be better educated and more well-to-do, which may have accounted for their lower risk.

What Other Health Benefits, If Any, Does Alcohol Have?

Even as little as one drink a week may protect against ischemic stroke (the most common type). Some research also suggests that moderate drinking may cut the risk of developing dementia, including Alzheimer's disease.

Is Wine a Better Choice Than Beer or Spirits?

It's almost certainly the alcohol that's protective, so it doesn't matter much which beverage you drink. Nevertheless, how you drink the beverage may be important. Beer and wine tend to accompany food—and food slows the absorption of alcohol, which is good. Furthermore, people who drink at meals, especially in the company of others, tend to keep intake moderate. Heavy drinkers usually drink outside of meals. It's true that wine (red or white) contains certain phytochemicals that may protect against heart disease or even cancer—and nonfermented grape juice also contains these compounds. Beer and spirits, made from grains and other plants, have phytochemicals of their own. Wine may simply seem healthier than other drinks because wine drinkers tend to be better educated and more prosperous than other drinkers, which means they tend to have better diets and better health care.

Isn't It Wine That Protects the French from Heart Disease—Even Though They Eat So Much Cheese?

Wine is only a small part of the picture. This is the famous "French paradox"—the French diet generally includes relatively high amounts of animal fat, but the French have lower rates of heart disease than Americans. Most important, though, the French tend to consume fewer calories and to be more active. And while the French have a lower death rate from heart disease, French life expectancy is only a year longer than that of Americans. In any case, wine consumption has been falling in France for decades, and half of all adults don't drink at all. It would be unwise to conclude from all this that drinking wine will make up for a diet high in calories and saturated fat.

Moderate intake is no more than one drink per day for a woman, on average, or two drinks for a man.

What Is "Moderation"?

This is a tricky question, and it varies according to your age and sex. The official definition of a "drink" is 12 ounces of beer, 4 to 5 ounces of wine, and 1.5 ounces of 80-proof spirits. Most people are surprised to learn that these all contain the same amount of pure alcohol, about half an ounce (a little more in the spirits). Moderate intake is no more than one drink per day for a woman, on average, or two drinks for a man. Most studies have found that people who drink this much have the lowest overall mortality rate—lower than non-drinkers, occasional drinkers, and heavy drinkers.

But, in fact, the studies diverge. The new one described in the first paragraph found higher intakes beneficial. Other studies have found lower intakes to be best. Moreover, if it's healthy for a man to have up to 14 drinks a week, can he drink six on Friday and six on Saturday and abstain the rest of the week? Probably not—binge drinking appears to be harmful. What about body size: is it okay for a tall man who weighs 200 pounds to drink more? What about an athletic woman that same size? Or a man 5'4" and thin? Even one drink can be too much for a very small woman. Obviously, size can sometimes trump gender, or at least confuse the issue. And age comes into play, too, since alcohol affects older people more.

Another problem: Portion inflation occurs not only on your plate, but in your glass. Many bars and restaurants do not serve standard-sized drinks, and what's served as one drink actually may be the equivalent of two or even three. Most people are pleased to be served generously—but you can't take half your drink home in a doggy bag, as you can your entree. If you ordinarily serve wine or spirits at home without measuring, it might be instructive to measure and see how close you come to the standard serving sizes. That will give you some idea, too, of how much you're getting in a restaurant.

Why Are the Guidelines Different for Men and Women?

Alcohol affects men and women differently. A woman will get more intoxicated than a man from the same amount of alcohol. Women tend to be smaller, with a lower percentage of water and a higher percentage of body fat. Since alcohol is distributed through body water and is more soluble in water than in fat, blood alcohol concentrations (BACs) in women tend to be higher. In addition, the stomach enzyme that breaks down alcohol before it reaches the bloodstream is less active in women. Alcohol also carries additional health risks for women, since heavy drinking boosts the risk of osteoporosis. Women are more prone to suffer liver damage from heavy drinking, too.

Is "Moderation" the Same for Older People?

The definition of moderate changes as you get older. Most experts think that after 65, moderation means half a drink a day for a woman, one drink for a man. If you're over 65, you probably can't hold your alcohol as well as you used to. That's because your body doesn't process alcohol as well, so you end up with a higher BAC than a younger person would. And you feel the effects more from a given BAC. Alcohol is doubly risky for hip fractures, too: not only does excessive drinking decrease bone density, it also increases the risk of falls in older people. Alcohol can interfere with many medications older people take, as well as increase age-related driving risks.

What About Breast Cancer?

The American Cancer Society lists alcohol as a risk factor for breast cancer, but most of the evidence concerns heavy drinking. Studies have yielded conflicting results about light to moderate drinking. Should a woman have a drink a day to ward off heart disease and forget about the possible breast cancer risk? Nobody should start drinking to protect the heart. But if you already have a drink a day, there's no health reason to quit, unless you know you are at high risk for breast cancer. Even then, the evidence is far from clear.

Why Does the American Cancer Society Recommend Restricting Alcohol or Abstaining?

Because even a moderate intake may increase the risk of cancers of the mouth, esophagus, liver, bladder, pancreas, and colon—besides the concern about breast cancer.

Wouldn't It Be Okay for a Pregnant or Nursing Woman to Drink Just a Small Amount?

If you are pregnant, trying to conceive, or nursing, you should abstain. Alcohol harms the fetus and the nursing infant, and is a leading cause of birth defects and mental retardation. No one has been able to determine if any level of intake—even one drink now and then—is safe.

Who, Besides Pregnant Women, Should Steer Clear of Alcohol?

- Anyone who is unable to drink moderately. This includes recovering alcoholics and possibly those with a strong family history of alcoholism.

- Anyone taking sedatives, sleeping pills, antidepressants, or anticonvulsants should get medical advice about whether these drugs can be safely combined with alcohol. Alcohol can interact with many other medications, too, including over-the-counter pain relievers. When you get a new prescription, ask whether it's okay to drink. With nonprescription medication, read the label carefully and abstain if necessary.

- Don't drink if you are planning to drive or operate machinery within the next few hours. If you have had a drink, don't get behind the wheel.

- Don't drink if you have uncontrolled hypertension, high blood levels of triglycerides, abnormal heart rhythms, peptic ulcers, or sleep apnea. If diagnosed with any disorder, talk to your doctor about the advisability of drinking.

What Are Other Risks of Heavy Drinking?

Heavy drinking increases the risk of liver disease, damage to the brain and pancreas, and hemorrhagic stroke. It can damage heart muscle. It increases the risk of falls, injuries, car crashes (often involving pedestrians who have been drinking), workplace injuries, firearms injuries, homicides, and suicides. It contributes to domestic violence and child abuse.

Should *Anybody* Start Drinking for Heart Benefits?

Few doctors think so, particularly since much is left to learn and alcohol is so risky. If you don't drink, for whatever reason, don't feel pressured to start. There are better ways to prevent heart disease: following a heart-healthy diet, exercising regularly and vigorously, not smoking, keeping your blood pressure under control, and losing weight if need be. On medical advice, you may also want to take low-dose aspirin and, if necessary, a cholesterol-lowering drug. If you already drink moderately, you are probably getting some additional benefit. But do consider your age, sex, and family history. Remember that "moderation" for a woman means no more than one drink a day, on average, two drinks for a man. And that if you are past 65, you should probably cut that amount in half.

3

Underage Drinking Leads to Risky Behavior and Alcohol Abuse

Kelly Dedel

Kelly Dedel is the director of One in 37 Research, Inc., a criminal justice consulting firm based in Portland, Oregon. She has provided evaluation-related technical assistance to more than sixty jurisdictions nationwide for the Bureau of Justice Assistance.

Despite the fact that drinking alcohol while under the age of twenty-one is against the law, teenagers are drinking at younger ages and engaging in riskier behaviors while under the influence of alcohol. These risky behaviors, such as drunk driving, disorderly conduct, acquaintance rape, vandalism, or assault, can lead to dire consequences. Researchers have found that many teenagers drink to relieve stress or to feel more socially confident, or simply because they think everyone else is doing it. And because young people report that it is very easy to obtain alcohol, increased enforcement of minimum-drinking-age laws is vital to reduce the harms associated with underage drinking.

Young people use alcohol more than any other drug, including tobacco. Underage drinking—that is, drinking under the age of 21—is prohibited throughout the United States. Despite a historical lack of vigorous enforcement, minimum-drinking-age laws have been very effective in reducing many

Kelly Dedel, "The Problem of Underage Drinking," *Underage Drinking*, Center for Problem-Oriented Policing, August 2010, pp. 1–12. Reproduced by permission.

of the harms associated with underage drinking, such as traffic fatalities and alcohol-related injuries, as well as assaults and other crimes. There is significant potential for further harm reduction if additional strategies targeting the factors underlying the problem are implemented.

Virtually all high school students and most college students are under 21. However, most drink alcohol at least occasionally, and many drink frequently and heavily. They can get alcohol for free or at low prices, which contributes to their drinking at levels that significantly increase their risk of negative alcohol-related consequences. The proportion of underage youth who drink has not changed significantly over the past decade in the United States. Indeed, if anything, they are starting to drink at a younger age, and their drinking patterns are becoming more extreme.

Negative Effects from Drinking Alcohol

Underage drinkers experience a wide range of alcohol-related health, social, criminal justice, and academic problems. They do not all experience the same level of problems—those who drink more, and drink more often, suffer a greater number of negative consequences. However, negative consequences occur across a wide range of consumption levels and frequencies.

Alcohol use contributes to property damage, rape, and other violent crime on college campuses.

Young drinkers report a range of negative effects from alcohol, all of which can lead to troubled interactions with others, particularly police officers or other responsible adults who try to intervene. These include the following:

- *Overconfidence and recklessness.* Excessive drinking may cause people to act in ways they would normally consider unwise or inappropriate.

- *Lack of awareness.* As people become intoxicated, they may not be fully aware of what is happening, and may not be able to figure out how to react to situations appropriately.

- *Aggression.* Drinkers may misread cues from other people as being offensive, and react violently.

- *Loss of control.* Drinkers' motor skills may become impaired, and drinkers may also lose control of their emotions.

These effects often lead young drinkers to come into contact with police, either as offenders or as victims. Youths who drink heavily are more likely to carry handguns than those who do not drink. Alcohol use contributes to property damage, rape, and other violent crime on college campuses, and about half of college crime victims have been drinking before the crime occurs. A significant proportion of young drivers killed in car accidents are intoxicated when the crash occurs.

Further, underage college students who drink heavily are more likely to miss class, fall behind in school, sustain an injury, have unplanned or unprotected sex, drive after drinking, or have contact with campus police. Students also experience "secondhand" effects of others' alcohol misuse, such as having their sleep or study time interrupted; having to take care of an intoxicated friend; being insulted or humiliated by drinkers; receiving unwanted sexual advances; getting in serious arguments; having their personal property damaged; being assaulted, sexually or otherwise; and being raped by an acquaintance. There are also a number of physical and mental health-related consequences of alcohol use. . . .

Very few college students experience any college-based disciplinary action as a result of their drinking, despite widespread use and serious consequences for the individuals, their peers, and their communities. The past decade has witnessed increased concern about and creativity in confronting the issue, and both adults and youths support measures to prevent underage drinking. . . .

Underage drinking is associated with a number of other problems:

- Drunken driving

- Speeding in residential areas

- Cruising

- Disorderly conduct in public places

- Assaults in and around bars

- Acquaintance rape

- House parties

- Rave parties

- Vandalism

- Noise complaints in residential areas.

Young people often go out intending to get drunk, and may try to intensify their drunkenness by drinking a lot very quickly.

Reasons Why Underage People Drink

Some researchers have found that drinking, particularly among underage college students, "is often so routine that people find it difficult to explain why they do it." However, there are several common themes that appear to underlie underage drinking. Many see drinking as a "rite of passage," or a fundamental part of adolescence and college life. Young people develop beliefs about the acceptability of underage drinking from their peers, parents, and other agents of informal social control. Many young people believe that drinking will make it easier to be part of a group, reduce tension, relieve stress, help them to forget their worries, increase their sexual attractiveness, or make them more socially confident. People who attribute such benefits to alcohol are more likely to drink than people who believe drinking has more negative consequences (e.g., loss of control, legal troubles, health problems).

Young people often go out intending to get drunk, and may try to intensify their drunkenness by drinking a lot very quickly or drinking especially strong liquor. However, many young people unintentionally get drunk when they misjudge their limits.

Many young people do not drink at all, or drink at minimal levels. Their decision not to drink or to drink in moderation appears to result from a combination of factors:

- *Attachment.* Young people with strong ties to family, friends, and significant others tend to drink less. They have close emotional ties with others, and care about others' expectations and opinions regarding their behavior.

- *Commitment.* Young people who invest significant amounts of time, energy, and resources in conventional activities such as studying, working, taking part in organized religion, and/or participating in clubs or athletics tend to drink less than students who are not so invested, perhaps because they have less time available for alcohol-focused activities.

- *Belief.* Young people who accept conventional values, obey society's rules, and respect authority tend to drink less than those who do not.

In addition, much research suggests that young people—college students in particular—drink because they assume everyone else does. Students consistently overestimate the amount that other students drink and the proportion of their fellow students who are heavy drinkers. Given that adolescents and young adults are susceptible to peer pressure and want to conform, it is likely that their perceptions of others' alcohol use influence their own drinking, whether or not their perceptions are correct.

Factors Contributing to Underage Drinking

Underage drinking occurs in an environment saturated by alcohol advertising on television, on billboards, at sporting and music events, and in national and local newspapers. The alcohol industry spends far more to promote its products than is spent on public messages encouraging responsible drinking. This media saturation may promote, facilitate, and perpetuate heavy drinking among young people. In addition, many products (e.g., alcopops, wine coolers) have hip, colorful, youth-oriented packaging and are likely to appeal mainly to young people.

In addition, young people, particularly those in college, are surrounded by outlets (e.g., grocery and convenience stores) that sell alcohol to be consumed elsewhere, or "off premises," as well as "on-premises" outlets such as bars and restaurants. High concentrations of alcohol outlets are associated with higher rates of heavy drinking and drinking-related problems among college students.

Alcohol outlets and advertisers team up to provide an additional incentive for underage drinking: price promotions and drink specials. In general, lower prices result in higher consumption levels across all age levels. Price promotions offer discounts for high-volume purchases, such as kegs and cases of beer. College campuses near retailers that sell large volumes of low-price alcohol have higher rates of binge drinking than those campuses near outlets that do not sell discount alcohol.

Many bars and restaurants have discount prices (e.g., during happy hour) and drink specials (e.g., two for one, ladies drink free) that encourage heavy drinking among all customers, some of whom may be underage.

Many high school and college students say that they attend parties or go out drinking because "there is nothing else to do." Like older adults, adolescents and young adults enjoy socializing and need a variety of avenues to interact with peers, make new friends, and pursue romantic relationships. In the absence of alcohol-free places to socialize, young people go to parties where alcohol is present, and may succumb to peer pressure to drink.

How Underage Drinkers Obtain Alcohol

Underage drinkers obtain alcohol from two main sources: third parties, such as legal-age friends, siblings, and strangers; and commercial outlets, such as stores, bars, and restaurants (often by using a fake ID).

Home is the primary source of alcohol among the youngest drinkers. Some youth take alcohol from their parents' liquor cabinets without their parents' knowledge. Some parents supply their underage children with alcohol at special events such as graduations, weddings, or holiday parties.

Underage drinkers sometimes ask strangers to buy alcohol for them, often in exchange for a fee or a portion of the alcohol purchased. This practice is called "shoulder tapping"—underage youth wait outside a store and tap a stranger on the shoulder to make the request.

Most underage drinkers report it is "very easy" to obtain alcohol; about one in four underage college students report that they can buy alcohol without age verification, or with a fake ID. Studies of alcohol purchases across the country reveal that, depending on the location and the environmental context, 40 to 90 percent of retail outlets have sold alcohol to underage buyers.

In some cases, retailers do not ask for ID. In others, underage drinkers present an ID card that has been altered to indicate they are of legal drinking age, or an ID card that belongs to someone who is of legal drinking age. The underage drinker may resemble the person in the photograph, or may substitute his or her own picture and relaminate the card. People can purchase fake IDs on the Internet, buy them directly from counterfeiters, or use fraudulent documents to get a driver's license. Recent advancements in technology have made the counterfeiting of state-issued ID cards easier, using a scanner and a color printer. Use of fake IDs is more common in urban areas and in states without consistent enforcement of underage purchase laws. Furthermore, young people are more likely to obtain and use a fake ID if they think their peers support the practice.

Where Underage Drinking Occurs

Underage people drink at a variety of locations, including the following:

- *Parties in private residences.* Large numbers of young people may gather in a home, often while the parents are away, or in a college student's off-campus residence. Parties in residential areas often generate complaints from neighbors who are disturbed by noise, improper parking, property damage, and littering. Such parties are of particular concern to police because they often include large numbers of underage drinkers and large quantities of alcohol. If the hosts charge an entry fee, they are essentially selling alcohol without a license, often to guests who are not of legal drinking age. House parties are popular among both high school and college students, as well as underage nonstudents. College students who live off campus are more likely to attend house parties than those who live on campus, and underage drinkers are more likely to gain access to alcohol at house parties than in bars or restaurants.

- *Parties at outdoor venues such as beaches, parks, fields, or parking lots.* The remoteness of these locations may reduce the chances that residents will be bothered, but also usually means that partygoers will have to drive home after drinking. These parties, like those in private residences, rarely provide nonalcoholic beverages or food to mitigate alcohol's intoxicating effects.

- *College campuses.* Many colleges and universities have on-campus bars and pubs, and social and athletic events at which alcohol sales are permitted. Of particular note is the high rate of underage and binge drinking that occurs at fraternity houses. Over the years, fraternity membership has become closely associated with heavy drinking, as part of social events, pledging, and initiations. Most students who join fraternities expect that alcohol will be central to their experience, despite the fact that most are underage. The high levels of drinking associated with fraternities are hazardous not only to members, but also to the large number of underage college or high school guests who regularly attend fraternity parties. Breaking up these parties and identifying the responsible adult can be particularly difficult for police.

- *Bars and restaurants.* Older underage drinkers are more likely to drink in bars and restaurants. Their close proximity to campus and advertised drink promotions make these venues an attractive choice for off-campus underage drinking. Many colleges have out-of-state students, requiring doormen or bartenders to judge the authenticity of driver's licenses with which they might not be familiar.

- *Special events.* Many colleges and communities have special events that seem to encourage widespread, heavy drinking, such as homecoming, graduation, pre- or post-semester parties, Halloween, Mardi Gras, and athletic events. Partly due to the large number of people present, and the failure of event planners to create specific "over 21 only" areas, underage people may have little difficulty getting alcohol through third-party purchases and drinking it unnoticed. In some cases, supervising adults both expect and tolerate underage drinking.

High school and college students often play any of hundreds of drinking games.

Spring break is a college ritual associated with excessive drinking and other high-risk, extreme behavior. One study of students visiting a Florida beach community during spring break found that 75 percent of the males reported being intoxicated at least once per day, while 40 percent of females reported the same. More than 50 percent of the men and more than 40 percent of the women reported drinking until they got sick or until they passed out at least once during the weeklong period. Given that people usually vomit when their body's blood alcohol content (BAC) reaches approximately 0.16, and lose consciousness at a BAC of approximately 0.30, it is clear that many students on spring break are drinking at unsafe levels.

In addition, high school and college students often play any of hundreds of drinking games. These games encourage heavy drinking, and the resulting inability to follow game rules leads to even more drinking.

4

Lowering the Legal Drinking Age Could Reduce Underage Alcohol Abuse

Choose Responsibility

Choose Responsibility, a nonprofit organization founded in 2007, advocates an accurate, unbiased, and reality-based approach to alcohol education developed and implemented on a state-by-state basis. The organization also believes federal legislation should not penalize states that choose to participate in alcohol education programs based on a minimum drinking age of eighteen.

Many researchers and experts claim that since the passage of the National Minimum Drinking Age Act in 1984, which standardized the legal drinking age at twenty-one in all states, the number of alcohol-related deaths for those between eighteen and twenty years of age has decreased. Other feasible explanations for that decrease, however, could be tougher prosecution and punishment for drunk driving, mandatory seatbelt laws, airbags, safer vehicles, and sobriety checkpoints. Furthermore, evidence shows that most eighteen- to twenty-year-olds ignore the law and drink alcohol. Lowering the legal drinking age to eighteen, along with mandatory completion of an intensive alcohol education course and licensing program, would be much more effective in reducing alcohol abuse in young people than would simply maintaining the status quo.

Choose Responsibility, "Frequently Asked Questions," www.ChooseResponsibility.org, 2007. Reproduced by permission.

On April 14, 1982, President Reagan established the Presidential Commission Against Drunk Driving (PCDD). This commission established 39 recommendations to curb what was perceived to be a drunken driving epidemic. Taken together, the 39 recommendations were intended to be a comprehensive approach with a goal of reducing the number of alcohol-related deaths on the nation's highways. Recommendation number eight concerned the Minimum Legal Purchasing Age, and said that all states should raise their drinking age to 21, lest they lose a certain percentage of federal highway dollars. Though the target of the Commission's recommendations was intended to be drunk driving across the adult population, the disproportionate amount of attention paid to establishing 21 as the national minimum drinking age shifted the nation's focus to young people's drinking. Exclusive interest in raising the drinking age marginalized the effect of the remaining 38 recommendations, among them suggestions to implement youth education programs, establish a massive public information campaign, and to increase penalties for convicted drunken drivers.

Two years later, on July 17, 1984, after extensive lobbying from groups such as MADD, President Reagan signed the National Minimum Drinking Age Act, effectively creating a national minimum drinking age of 21.

Mothers Against Drunk Driving (MADD; then called Mothers Against Drunk Drivers) was founded by Candy Lightner in response to the 1980 death of her young daughter upon being struck by a repeat offense drunk driver. The organization and Lightner's testimony during Senate subcommittee hearings on the bill played an indispensable role in generating support from Congress, President Reagan and the general public for a standardized, nationwide 21-year-old drinking age.

The Current Law Causes a Lack of Consistency

Currently, the Federal Law provides for the following exceptions under the original legislation:

> ... the possession of alcohol for an established religious purpose; when accompanied by a parent, spouse or legal guardian age 21 or older; for medical purposes when prescribed or administered by a licensed physician, pharmacist, dentist, nurse, hospital or medical institution; in private clubs or establishments; or to the sale, handling, transport, or service in dispensing of any alcoholic beverage pursuant to lawful employment of a person under the age of twenty-one years by a duly licensed manufacturer, wholesaler, or retailer of alcoholic beverages.

In effect, this provision means that states that legislate one or more exceptions to the 21-year-old drinking age are not at risk of losing federal highway funding. This results in a lack of nationwide consistency in the laws governing alcohol use for people under age 21; for example, in many states, consumption of alcohol is not prohibited outright. As of 2006, 21 states have exceptions to the law for the consumption of alcohol by those under 21 and 28 states have exceptions that pertain to the furnishing of alcohol to those under 21. . . .

The Current Law Has Not Reduced Fatalities

Many studies confirm that since the drinking age was standardized at 21 in 1984, the overall number of alcohol-related fatalities for those aged 18–20 has decreased. However, this pattern of decline began in the early 1970s, years before passage of the National Minimum Drinking Age Act. Though organizations like MADD claim the 21-year-old drinking age has saved over 21,000 lives since the mid-1980s, it is impossible to assert a cause and effect relationship between the change in the law and the decline in alcohol-related traffic fatalities; many other factors, such as safer vehicles and more stringent drunk driving laws have played an undeniably important role. Several scholars have also presented the important argument that while deaths on the road may have declined sharply among 18–20-year-olds in the years following enactment of the 21-year-old drinking age, the slowest rate of decline and greatest number of annual fatalities is seen each year in the 21–24 age group. In 2002, for example, *twice* as many 21-year-olds died in alcohol-related auto accidents as 18-year-olds. Such a staggering statistic speaks volumes: a policy that claims to be saving thousands of lives each year may simply be re-distributing deaths over the life cycle to the point at which it becomes legal to drink alcohol—age 21.

Furthermore, for all alcohol related fatalities not associated with automobiles, raising the drinking age to 21 has had no discernible effect on fatalities associated with alcohol. Alcohol-related suicides, accidents, drownings, murders, and alcohol poisoning rates have shown no decline associated with the drinking age. Death or injury from alcohol overdose has become a great concern to parents, teachers, high school and college administrators since the drinking age was raised to 21.

Many Factors Contributed to the Decline in Fatalities

During the 1980s and 1990s, legislative changes, increased law enforcement, tougher prosecution and punishment, highly visible advocacy, and public education were all components of the "war on drunk driving." Other legislative changes, such as mandatory seat belt laws, lower BAC [blood alcohol content] limits, and stricter rules on automobile safety standards can also be credited. The decline in alcohol-related fatalities seen in the United States over the past two and a half decades is attributable to a combination of factors, including but not limited to safer vehicles, increased public awareness of the danger of drunk driving, use of designated drivers—a term that did not exist before the drinking age was raised—sobriety checkpoints, zero-tolerance laws for young drivers, and altogether more stringent enforcement of alcohol-impaired driving laws have led to the reduction seen in rates of drunk driving and related deaths. In fact, many of these improvements can be traced to the 39 recommendations presented by the Presidential Commission Against Drunk Driving in 1982. According to an analysis by NHTSA [National Highway Traffic Safety Administration], safety belts and air bags have had a vastly greater effect in preventing fatalities than the 21-year-old drinking age; for example, in 2002 and 2003 alone, more lives on the road were saved by the use of safety belts and airbags than there were in the entire history of the 21-year-old drinking age.

It is unlikely that a lower drinking age would increase rates of alcohol abuse.

Interventions over the past twenty years have succeeded not only in reducing the incidence of impaired driving and the crashes and fatalities that can result from it, but also in changing the norms related to driving after drinking. Drunken driving is no longer generally accepted in society, giving rise to designated drivers and fewer drunk drivers on today's roads. . . .

It is unlikely that a lower drinking age would increase rates of alcohol abuse. Although a significant body of literature suggests that an early onset of alcohol use is correlative with alcohol abuse later in life, the same literature also indicates no significant difference in rates of alcohol abuse between those who start drinking at 18, 19, 20 or 21. Those young people who begin to drink in early adolescence are more likely to end up with alcohol use problems later in life. It would still be just as illegal for young teens to drink, but under the new law there would be incentives for not using alcohol until one is 18 and punishments for those who choose to break the law.

Mandatory Licensing and Education Offer a Better Approach

In order to act as functional social policy, any attempt to lower the drinking age would need to be accompanied by provisions intended to keep alcohol away from young people under 18. Instead of lowering the drinking age to 18 and automatically allowing 18-year-olds all the privileges enjoyed now by those 21 and older, a better approach may be to regulate alcohol use by those 18–20 years of age through a graduated licensing system. This could consist of a period following an individual's eighteenth birthday in which he or she could drink only under the supervision of a parent or guardian. That individual could then pay a fee reflective of the program's implementation cost and enroll in a state-administered alcohol education course. Upon successful completion of the course requirements, an alcohol license would be issued, allowing that individual to consume alcohol within the confines of the law.

Those over 18 can make healthy, informed decisions when armed with the right information.

In order to prevent minors' ease of access to alcohol, anyone who chooses to enroll in the course must have successfully completed secondary education. Furthermore, anyone with an alcohol license who is caught driving while intoxicated, furnishing alcohol to minors, or in violation of any other provision of the law would have his or her license and all drinking privileges revoked until reaching age 21. . . .

If developed and implemented correctly, a mandatory alcohol education course would present new drinkers with a successful model for responsible and moderate behavior. By avoiding the pitfalls encountered by previous alcohol education programs—especially those that stress complete abstinence, the costs incurred as a result of alcohol-related crime and accidents, or the negative and addictive qualities of alcohol—such a program could define and model responsible use. Instead of highlighting the negative consequences of consumption and stigmatizing any and all alcohol use, an effective program would provide guidelines for healthy ways to consume alcohol, discourage drinking to the point of intoxication, and clearly outline both the negative and positive social and personal effects of drinking. The program would also be accompanied by a clear presentation of drinking laws and penalties for their violation. Provided to all newly enfranchised drinkers, the course information would present a viable, socially acceptable alternative to binge and goal-oriented drinking—the two activities that lead most often to auto accidents, crime, and overdose.

Above and beyond the content of the course, the effectiveness of an alcohol education program is contingent upon treating its subjects as adults. The existence of such a course would serve as acknowledgement of the fact that those over 18 can make healthy, informed decisions when armed with the right information. For many adolescents, alcohol is a vehicle for social rebellion, its abuse a function of asserting one's independence from infantilizing social policies. An alcohol education course would help normalize society's treatment of alcohol and its users.

There is overwhelming evidence which shows that the vast majority of 18–20 year olds choose to ignore the law and drink anyway. Unfortunately, since these young adults are breaking the law, they choose to drink in clandestine locations to avoid prosecution. This promotes unsafe and irresponsible drinking and has led to the development of a dangerous subculture among today's youth defined by drinking games, "pregaming," and large, out-of-control parties whose sole focus is drinking beyond the point of intoxication.

An 18-year-old drinking age would effectively remove young adults' drinking from secretive and dangerous locations.

Should the legal drinking age be lowered to 18, the privilege to drink would be contingent upon completion of an intensive alcohol education course specifically aimed at reducing at-risk drinking and promoting responsible, safe consumption. Because young adults would no longer have to drink behind closed doors to avoid getting caught, their formative encounters with alcohol would be in supervised, controlled environments. An 18-year-old drinking age would effectively remove young adults' drinking from secretive and dangerous locations.

A graduated licensing system has the potential to restrict the transfer of alcohol from 18-year-olds to younger teens. After a period of being permitted to drink only under parental supervision, 18-year-olds would then be allowed to enroll in an extensive alcohol education course, earning a drinking license upon successful completion. Individuals would be prevented from enrolling in the course until finishing secondary education.

Furthermore, any violation of the state's alcohol control laws, such as furnishing to minors or driving under the influence of alcohol, would result in immediate suspension of the drinking license. Young people caught drinking before they reach age 18 and obtain a license would be delayed from enrolling in the alcohol education course for a specified period of time. . . .

The combination of incentive and reward offered by the education and licensing program promises positive effects for those under and over 18 alike. Penalties for violation of alcohol control laws will encourage younger adolescents to abstain until they reach age 18; at the same time, those laws will encourage those over 18 who choose to drink to do so responsibly, so as to avoid revocation of their drinking license. Perhaps most importantly, though, this proposal will re-involve parents, teachers, and other role models in the process of teaching young adults how to drink in moderation. Marginalized under the current law, these figures would again be legally permitted to introduce young adults to alcohol consumption in the home and other safe, supervised locations.

The reality of the present drinking age is that it is ineffective in keeping alcohol out of the hands of underage drinkers.

The Responsible Use of Alcohol Will Reduce Risky Behavior

Advocates of a 21-year-old drinking age claim that lowering the drinking age would lead to several public health problems. Their concerns are twofold: increased rates of alcohol abuse and decreased mental faculties amongst new drinkers.

If the present 21-year-old drinking age were actually effective in reducing underage drinking in the 18–20 year-old cohort, then lowering the drinking age to 18 could very well increase rates of alcohol abuse. The logic is that a lower drinking age would provide access to alcohol to otherwise abstinent, but, potential abusers. However, the reality of the present drinking age is that it is ineffective in keeping alcohol out of the hands of underage drinkers, specifically those who are already in college, ages 18–20. Albeit misguided, the argument concerning the risk-prone nature of young adults is an important one. If the drinking age were lowered, it would give colleges and universities, and foremost parents, the opportunity to promote the healthy use of alcohol and provide a safe and supervised setting for young adults to consume alcohol. In terms of controlling and forestalling risky behavior, such an environment would be a vast improvement over the basements, dorm rooms, and fraternity houses where risky drinking behavior currently takes place. Secondly, if consuming alcohol before the age of 21 does have a deleterious effect on the cognitive abilities of drinkers, should there not be an entire generation of Americans that came of age from 1973–1984, even whole continents of people (Europe, most of Asia, Latin America, and Oceania), who are less intelligent, or cognitively impaired because of their early exposure to alcohol? The premise of such an argument is so outlandish, in fact, that no such study has ever been conducted.

We are faced with a law that is out of step with our cultural attitudes towards alcohol.

In the more than two decades that have passed since its implementation, the 21-year-old drinking age has created a climate in which terms like "binge" and "pregame" have come to describe young peoples' choices about alcohol; in which the law is habitually and thoughtlessly ignored by adolescents and adults alike; in which colleges and communities across the nation are plagued with out-of-control parties, property damage, and belligerent drunks; in which emergency rooms and campus health centers are faced with an alarming number of sometimes fatal cases of alcohol poisoning and overdose on weekend nights; and in which the role of parents in teaching responsible behavior around alcohol has been marginalized and the family disenfranchised. Maintaining status quo in America today is not an option.

We are faced with a law that is out of step with our cultural attitudes towards alcohol, one which encourages violation and breeds disrespect. Historically, we know that during the Vietnam War the 26th Amendment in 1971 provided 18-

year-olds the right to vote, the age at which one could be drafted to fight in the war. This constitutional recognition of 18-year-olds as consenting adults was fundamental for guaranteeing the right for 18-year-olds to drink. Again, a quarter century later, we are engaged in a war where many of the soldiers currently serving abroad are under the legal drinking age of 21. And while that historical parallel itself does not provide justification for changing the drinking age, it makes strikingly clear the poor logic behind the assumption that at the age of 18 one is too immature for alcohol consumption. If the drinking age were lowered, it would signal a transformation in the relationship our society has with its young adults. Besides engendering greater respect for the law, a lower and more easily enforced drinking age would offer alternative choices for parents and college campuses around the country in shaping responsible drinking behaviors and encouraging informed decisions about alcohol use.

5

Maintaining the Legal Drinking Age of 21 Curbs Underage Alcohol Abuse

Karen Arnold-Burger

Karen Arnold-Burger was a presiding judge of the Overland Park Municipal Court in Kansas and has been a judge of the Kansas Court of Appeals since January 6, 2011.

Many people wonder why we do not lower the legal drinking age to eighteen, if teens and twenty-year-olds are drinking alcohol despite the fact that it is against the law. There are many compelling reasons to maintain the legal drinking age at twenty-one: raising the drinking age to twenty-one is credited with saving thousands of young drivers' lives; lowering the drinking age would merely make alcohol available to even younger teens; alcohol can seriously damage the brain of an adolescent; and the earlier youth begin drinking alcohol, the more likely they are to become addicted. Yes, many teens ignore the law and drink alcohol, but studies show that the problems would be much worse if the drinking age were lowered.

"We can't stop kids from drinking, so why don't we just lower the drinking age back down to 18? They are adults for all other purposes. Eighteen-year-olds can vote, smoke, marry, drive, fly, pay taxes, take out loans, hold public office, serve on a jury and fight for their country, so what's the big deal? Let's stop spending all this tax money and law enforcement officer time fighting a losing battle!"

Karen Arnold-Burger, "The Top Five Reasons We Should Keep the Drinking Age at 21," Regional Prevention Center of Johnson, Leavenworth and Miami Counties, August 26, 2008. Reproduced by permission of the author.

I often hear this refrain as I speak to adults in our community. In fact, many Kansas parents today grew up in an era in Kansas when they could drink 3.2% beer when they were 18. Why did that change and should it be changed back? Some believe that allowing drinking at younger ages would mitigate youthful desire for alcohol as a "forbidden fruit" Before I share my "top five" reasons we should keep the drinking age at 21, let's take a little trip back in time and examine how the current law came to be.

The History Behind the Current Law

After Prohibition was repealed in 1933, the decision as to what the legal drinking age should be was left up to each individual state. Until 1970, the minimum drinking age in most states was 21. As part of the war protests of the 1960's, youth started lobbying for a lowered voting age and a lowered drinking age. *"Old Enough to Fight. . .Old Enough to Vote"* was on popular bumper stickers and buttons of the era. In 1971, the 26⁰ Amendment was adopted, lowering the voting age to 18 and drinking ages likewise started to be lowered around the country. Between 1970 and 1976, 21 states reduced the minimum drinking age to 18. Another 8 reduced it to 19 or 20. However, these states immediately noticed sharp increases in alcohol-related fatalities among teenagers and young adults. As a result, of the 29 states that had lowered their drinking age, 24 raised the age again between 1976 and 1984. By 1984, only three states allowed 18-year-olds to drink all types of alcoholic liquor. The others adopted some sort of stair-step age requirement based on the type of liquor being consumed.

Federal transportation authorities viewed this hodge-podge of state laws as a real highway traffic safety problem. Alcohol-related traffic injuries and fatalities were increasing and some of this was as a result of kids traveling from their home states to neighboring states that had lower drinking ages and then becoming injured or killed as they returned to their home states. These became known as "blood borders." In 1984, Congress enacted the *National Minimum Drinking Age Act* which had been recommended by President Reagan's Commission on Drunk Driving. States were threatened with the loss of 10% of their federal highway funds if they did not raise the minimum drinking age in their state to 21 for all alcoholic beverages. All states eventually complied so that now all 50 states have a minimum drinking age of 21. So, that brings us immediately to reason number one.

Increasing the minimum drinking age to 21 is credited with having saved 18,220 lives on the nation's highways between 1975 and 1998.

Reasons to Keep the Drinking Age at 21

1. 21 Saves Lives.

There is now a substantial body of scientific evidence showing that raising the minimum drinking age in 1984 directly resulted in reduced alcohol-related crashes and fatalities among young people as well as deaths from suicide, homicide, and non-vehicle unintentional injuries. According to the National Highway Traffic Safety Administration, increasing the minimum drinking age to 21 is credited with having saved 18,220 lives on the nation's highways between 1975 and 1998. Other studies have found that it is responsible for a 19% net decrease in fatal crashes involving young drivers, and is currently responsible for saving approximately 1,000 young lives each year.

2. The Brain Does Not Fully Develop until At Least 21.

More and more research has been released in recent years concerning the stages of brain development. We have learned that the brain does not finish developing until a person is in their early twenties. It appears that it is not coincidental that fatalities increase as the drinking age is lowered. Brain maturation culminates in the prefrontal cortex. This is the area that controls judgments and weighing risks and consequences. Previously, this area was thought to be fully mature by the age of 18. Studies now suggest that this area is not fully developed until around the age of 25. What does this mean? Those under the age of 25 are more likely to engage in thrill seeking activity, and less able to appreciate the consequences of risky behavior. This new research has legislators around the country examining things like raising the driving age and raising the age at which a person can be executed for a crime committed during these "formative" years. Alcohol impairs judgment and heightens risk-taking behavior as well as slowing perceptual and motor skills, so given to a person who has an immature brain function in these areas already, research shows that the effects are even more exaggerated. And finally, the research indicates that alcohol or drug use during these formative years can cause long term, irreversible damage.

The explicit aim of existing policy is to delay underage alcohol use as long as possible.

---

3. The Longer We Can Delay Alcohol Use, the Better the Chance that a Person Will Never Have a Problem with Alcohol.

Alcoholism is a serious medical and social problem in this country. Criminal justice experts estimate that at least 75–80% of defendants involved in felony crimes or serious misdemeanors were either under the influence of alcohol or drugs when they committed their crime or committed their crime to obtain money to obtain alcohol or drugs or to to survive because they have lost their financial resources due to their addiction. Decrease in work productivity due to absenteeism, divorce, suicide, increased medical problems, school dropout rates and traffic collisions are just a few of the costs associated with alcoholism. Drug addiction rarely begins as such, but often begins as early onset alcohol use as the gateway for further experimentation. For every year we delay the onset of drinking, studies have shown we substantially increase the likelihood that our child will never have a problem with alcohol or drugs. Never. We know that alcohol use affects an adolescent brain differently than it does an adult. We know that because of this addiction onset can occur much sooner in a teenager (6–18 months) than an adult (5 years). The explicit aim of existing policy is to delay underage alcohol use as long as possible and, even if use begins, to reduce its frequency and quantity as much as possible.

10th–12th graders in states with lower drinking ages drank significantly more, were drunk more often, and were less likely to abstain from alcohol.

---

4. The Policy Does Work, Preventing "Low-Hanging Fruit."

Allowing drinking at younger ages would not mitigate youthful desire for alcohol as a "forbidden fruit" it would merely make alcohol more available to an even younger population, replacing "forbidden fruit" with "low-hanging fruit." The practices and behaviors of 18-year-olds are particularly influential on 15–17 year-olds. If 18-year-olds get the OK to drink, they will be modeling drinking for younger teens. Legal access to alcohol for 18-year-olds will provide more opportunities for younger teens to obtain it illegally from older peers.

We do have the benefit of some studies that were done before the drinking age was raised nationwide in 1984. The 1978 *National Study of Adolescent Drinking Behavior* found that 10th–12th graders in states with lower drinking ages drank significantly more, were drunk more often, and were less likely to abstain from alcohol. Additionally, national data show that high school seniors who could not legally drink until age 21 drank less before age 21 and between ages 21–25 than did students in states with lower drinking ages. Countries with lower drinking ages suffer from alcohol-related problems similar to, and in some cases worse than, those in the U.S.

Certainly, the large numbers of current underage drinkers breeds frustration, but the studies show that the numbers would be much worse if the drinking age were lowered.

5. Department of Defense Regulations Allow Members of the Active Military Who Are Under 21 to Consume Alcohol in Controlled Situations.

And what about this "*Old Enough to Fight . . . Old Enough to Drink*" argument? Well, the fact is, if your child has volunteered to serve in the military, when the going gets tough, there is a good chance he or she will be allowed to have a drink.

In the "old days" anyone on active military duty could consume alcohol on military installations, regardless of the legal drinking age off-base. However, in the mid-80's federal law was changed requiring military installation commanders to adopt the same drinking age as the state the military base is located in. At all oversees military installations, the drinking age is 18 unless international treaties or agreements mandate a higher age. So if your child is risking his or her life overseas, and there is no treaty prohibiting alcohol on base, he or she may drink at 18.

In addition, the commander of a military installation may waive the drinking age requirements state-side, if such commander determines that the exemption is justified by special circumstances. Special circumstances are those infrequent, non-routine military occasions when an entire unit, as a group, marks at a military installation a uniquely military occasion such as the conclusion of arduous military duty or the anniversary of the establishment of a military service or organization. The event must be held on a military installation. The commander is required to ensure that appropriate controls are in place to prevent endangering military service members or the surrounding community.

Therefore, the fact that an 18-year-old can serve in the military does not negate all the other reasons the drinking age should remain at 21 for those who choose not to volunteer for such a dangerous assignment.

In conclusion, ages of initiation vary in this country—one may vote at 18, drink at 21, visit the local casino at 21, rent a car at 25, and run for president at 35. These ages may appear arbitrary, but they take into account the requirements, risks, and benefits of each act. The national minimum legal drinking age of 21 has survived the test of time and is firmly supported by current scientific research. The lives and futures of our children depend on its continued support.

6

Alcoholism Is a Brain Disease

Katherine Eban and Larkin Warren, with others

Katherine Eban is an award-winning reporter who has contributed to Fortune, Self, Vanity Fair, *the* New York Times, New York, *and several national television and radio news programs. Larkin Warren is a former editor of* Esquire, Good Housekeeping, *the* American Benefactor, Lear's *and* Travel Holiday, *and a contributor to various magazines and literary journals.*

Contrary to what many people believe—that alcoholics are simply weak-willed and of low moral character—alcohol addiction is a disease. Like other diseases, alcoholism affects the health and well-being of the addict and can be managed with the proper treatment. Breakthroughs in technology have allowed researchers to examine how the brain works and to examine closely the neurotransmitters and the biochemical response systems of the brain. Such high-tech scanning has resulted in new understanding that alcoholism is in fact a chronic brain disease.

Addiction is a complex disease. It has profound effects on the health and well-being of the individual addict, as well as those around them, and society at large. Like other chronic illnesses, addiction—with the proper treatment—can be managed, so that an addict can live a life without drugs. The road to recovery, however, is often fraught with devastating consequences, some of which are short-lived and others, lifelong. Health, reputation, livelihood, and interpersonal relationships

Katherine Eban and Larkin Warren, with David Sheff, Chris Jozefowicz, Elizabeth Dougherty, and Lynora Williams, *Addiction: Why Can't They Just Stop?: New Knowledge, New Treatments, New Hope*, edited by John Hoffman and Susan Froemke, Emmaus, PA: Rodale, 2007, pp. 29, 32–35, 47, 53–65. Reproduced by permission.

are just a few areas that can be severely affected by drug and alcohol abuse—and that, in many cases, can be repaired in recovery.

Today's epidemic of addiction to drugs or alcohol is a subject that is talked about candidly only with extreme difficulty. Why? The stigma and shame associated with drug and alcohol dependence have helped to build an invisible wall that can isolate addicts and their loved ones in times of deep crisis. Common misconceptions as to both the causes of addiction and the ways in which it can be successfully (or not) treated add to the fog of mystery and confusion. . . .

Addiction was first defined as a disease by the American Medical Association in 1956.

A Chronic, Relapsing Brain Disease

Each addict leaves a unique footprint on their family and community. Depending on who the addicts are, what they're using, how they get it, and the behavior the addiction encourages—erratic mood swings, manic spending, inexplicable fears, sullen apathy, spousal abuse, petty theft, the list goes on—the impact of the addiction can range from quietly devastating to openly dangerous. Whether it's the child addict whose habit upends her family's ability to get through the day or the hooked adult who commits crimes to support his fix, every addict spreads tentacles of consequences through their home and neighborhood. Yet the problem remains cloaked in shame, denial, and stigma, discussed in hushed tones, as if the people who suffer from the disease are somehow responsible for it. After all, addicts invited this particular problem on themselves, didn't they?

Well, yes. And no. Addiction was first defined as a disease by the American Medical Association in 1956, and it has taken a full half-century of research and treatment for even medical and psychological professionals to shed old beliefs. So perhaps it should come as no surprise that society at large has difficulty seeing an old disease in a new way.

Addicts are weak, the myth goes. Weak of mind, weak of character. Or they're willfully self-destructive. Or they're unbearably selfish. They must be. Otherwise they'd stop hurting themselves and hurting others as well, right? "That's the real mistake that people make," says senior research psychologist Dennis. "They think it's about a morality play, a moral shortcoming. That somehow you've failed as a person."

Repeated use of drugs and alcohol alters the way the brain works.

According to a recent survey by the National Council on Alcoholism and Drug Dependence, half the public believes that addiction is a personal weakness. In the 2006 *USA Today/HBO Family Drug Addiction Poll*, while 76 percent of those polled identified addiction as a "disease," they identified "lack of willpower" as the main problem facing addicts.

In fact, the new understanding of drug and alcohol addiction that top scientists like [Nora] Volkow [director of the National Institute on Drug Abuse (NIDA)] and [Mark] Willenbring [of the National Institute on Alcohol Abuse and Alcoholism (NIAAA)] agree on suggests the opposite. A more accurate way to put it would be that any so-called lack of willpower in an addict has been caused by changes in the brain. Dependence on drugs or alcohol caused these very changes. The inability to make clear decisions is a by-product of the same disease from which the addict is trying to escape. What could be more insidious? More clearly than ever, today's addiction specialists understand this conundrum: repeated use of drugs and alcohol alters the way the brain works. These alterations can now be observed and described in precise detail. The sea change in our understanding of addiction has begun to yield new treatments, including new types of medications that help restore the brain's normal functions. The first step, therefore, is to call addiction what it is, instead of the well-worn metaphors that polite, embarrassed, or justifiably frightened people have used for generations. It is not a "problem." It is not "a phase she's going through." It is not "shaking out the jams before he settles down." It is a chronic, relapsing brain disease. . . .

The Addicted Brain: Far Beyond Willpower

What Volkow and others have discovered (or perhaps more accurately, reaffirmed and given new meaning to) bears repeating: addiction is a progressive, chronic, relapsing disorder of the brain. Addiction *can* be successfully treated. It is not a moral failing but something much closer in its nature to diseases like asthma or diabetes.

"The science of understanding addiction has just been exploding in recent years through the use of any number of different technologies, including genetics, animal studies, studies in humans, and brain imaging," says NIAAA's Willenbring. "We are really starting to piece together some of the brain mechanisms involved in the development of and resolution of drug dependence and alcohol dependence." Such advances mean a new ability to objectively measure the success of different treatments and to develop new treatments that can be clinically proven to work. This watershed moment promises to help sweep away decades of moralistic cant and punitive condemnation surrounding the fate of addicts in this country. No longer should addicts be expected to just tough it out when the true, slippery nature of their disease can be so much more finely calibrated. . . .

"Patients say, 'Why can't I just stop? I've lost so much, I've paid such a high price,'" says Anna Rose Childress of the University of Pennsylvania. "Parents say, 'They've completely wrecked their lives. Our lives, too. Why can't they just stop?'

What we're beginning to understand now, at the level of the brain, is that there are lots of cards that are stacked in the wrong direction here."

Most people typically have three or four false starts before they're able to successfully maintain a year of sobriety.

When the primary focus of someone's life is getting and using a substance that alters their way of thinking, everything else eventually falls by the wayside. Personal relationships are strained, education is interrupted or ended, and bills go unpaid. Add to this list any number of untreated physical and mental illnesses, and a potentially crippling social isolation.

And that's just the damage we can see. Unseen is the actual biochemical alteration of the parts of the brain that are necessary for us to make decisions and control our behavior. That's why, even when an addict has a strong desire to change their life, what happens next is not as simple as walking into the first AA [Alcoholics' Anonymous] meeting they find. "They can't stop because their brain has been changed," says David Rosenbloom, PhD, director of Join Together, a program of the Boston University School of Public Health. "Most people typically have three or four false starts before they're able to successfully maintain a year of sobriety," reports Michael Dennis of Chestnut Health Systems. "That can often take eight or nine years."

Recovery is possible, but it can depend to a great degree on how old the person is who comes to treatment, how long they have been using, to what degree their addiction may be complicated by co-occurring mood and anxiety disorders, and what substances, or combinations of substances, they have been using. "The brain has a tremendous capacity for recovery, because it's what we call 'plastic,'" says NIDA's Volkow. "But as we grow older, we lose some of the plasticity of the brain necessary for recovery."

Recovery is a process far more complicated and complex than just ending the use of chemical substances; it involves the rewiring of brain circuits altered by drugs or alcohol. However, there are significant barriers to that process, one of them being the longstanding stigma against addiction and the person who suffers from it.

"Addicts are discriminated against in ways that people suffering from no other disease are," says Rosenbloom. "It starts with a healthcare system that doesn't cover the disease very well. And [because] many addicts have been in the criminal justice system, they can't get jobs. We throw them out of public housing. They can't get welfare, they can't get food stamps for their kids."

As with almost all forms of discrimination, this one carries a big price tag, both to the individual and to society. And just as we've learned with other forms of discrimination, the only way to reverse this one is with knowledge. We must understand not just what addiction does to the lives of the addict, their loved ones, and the population overall, but what it is—a brain disease.

Addicts are discriminated against in ways that people suffering from no other disease are.

"One of the exciting things about this moment, in terms of our understanding addiction, is that for the first time in all of human history we can peek inside the brain and see what may be broken," explains Childress. "And if we can see what's broken, we have an idea how to go about fixing it."

Inside the brain, the actual neurological response to alcohol and drug consumption (and the effects of addiction) can clearly be seen. And we do mean *seen*, in vivid, multicolored, multidimensional images relayed by high-tech scanning machines. In the past several years, scientists have learned more about how the human brain works than in all the previous centuries, primarily because of the development of a series of machines that allow them to look inside a living brain while the brain's owner is awake and responsive to stimuli.

Different types of messenger chemicals inside the brain, called neurotransmitters, carry information from one brain cell, or neuron, to another. Imaging technologies can reflect the activity in these transmitter systems, measuring how well (or how poorly) they do their jobs when alcohol or drugs have affected the brain. Some of the key neurotransmitters whose communication functions are disrupted by abused substances are dopamine, serotonin, GABA [gamma-Aminobutyric acid], and glutamate. And while all drugs of abuse directly or indirectly affect dopamine, there are also specific drug effects on other neurotransmitter systems. For example, LSD [lysergic acid diethylamide] and Ecstasy alter serotonin function; heroin and morphine affect opiate receptors; and alcohol interacts with almost every neurotransmitter, but especially GABA and glutamate.

"Go!": The Dopamine Pleasure Pathway

Research has shown that all drugs of abuse directly or indirectly activate the brain's pleasure pathway, the intricate network that controls and regulates our ability to feel pleasure. When we experience something good—lovemaking, a good meal, a beautiful sunset—our brain experiences a surge in the level of the neurotransmitter dopamine. We feel warm, calm, and happy. After awhile, dopamine returns to a baseline level, and we go about our lives, looking forward to the next pleasurable experience.

We look forward to the next time because the experience is logged into the brain's limbic system, which, in addition to being the center for pleasure and emotion, houses key memory and motivation circuits. This is what the brain's dopamine pathway does; it records both the actual experience of pleasure and ensures that the behaviors that led to it are remembered and repeated. In between pleasurable events, there is a quiet period when the neurotransmitters return to their baseline levels. It is useful to remember that the whole system evolved from the biological imperative of survival. Food meant survival, sex meant survival, and going back for more of both meant survival of the species, in the most literal sense.

The first time we experience a drug or alcohol high, the amount of chemical we ingest often exceeds (by a factor of anywhere from two to ten) the levels of naturally occurring neurotransmitters in our body. Dopamine levels may spike higher than they do even with eating, and that initial spike typically lasts longer. That experience, no matter how brief, is stored in the hippocampus and amygdala, important centers of motivation that are sometimes called the "Go!" system. Getting drunk with your buddies, getting high at the beach— they both initially flood the brain with dopamine, along with a picture-memory of the event and the body's pleasurable response to it. And so we look forward to doing it again.

But it's a trick.

After each upward spike, dopamine levels again recede, eventually to below the baseline. The following spike doesn't go quite as high as the one before it. Over time, the rush becomes smaller, and the crash that follows becomes deeper. The brain has been fooled into "thinking" that achieving that high is equivalent to survival (even more so than with food and sex), and the "Go!" light is on all the time. Eventually, the brain is forced to turn on a self-defense mechanism, reducing the production of dopamine altogether—and weakening the pleasure circuit's function. At this point, the addicted person is compelled to use the substance not to get high, but to feel "normal"—since there's little or no dopamine response to be had. It is like repeatedly jamming your ATM card in the slot even though your bank account has been long since overdrawn.

"Stop!": The Brain's Brakes

In addition to the "Go!" system, the brain also has a built-in "Stop!" system: the prefrontal cortex, sometimes referred to as the seat of sober second thought. With this system, we pull all the information together, weigh it, examine the risks and consequences, and strategize the next move. Is this a good idea? Is this illegal or immoral, or will it make me sick? Will I be able to drive safely, will I be too hung over to get to my job in the morning?

"When things are working right, the 'Go!' circuitry and the 'Stop!' circuitry really are interconnected and are talking to each other to help you weigh the consequences of a decision and decide when to go or not to go," says Childress. "It's not that they're separable. They're interactive. They're interlinked at all times."

With addicts, however, "it is as though [the systems] have become functionally disconnected. It is as though the 'Go!' system is sort of running off on its own, is a rogue system now and is not interacting in a regular, seamless, integrated way with the 'Stop!' system," Childress says.

Successful addiction recovery truly involves a rewiring of the brain.

Drugs of abuse directly activate the pleasure pathway, but recent research shows that addiction also involves the same pathways that manage memory and learning; that is, the addictive process moves in, undoes or weakens what the brain knew before, and then teaches it something else entirely. One amazing illustration of how this works is with Childress's patient William, a longtime cocaine addict in supervised recovery. When William undergoes a PET [positron emission tomography] scan and is shown images of a beautiful sunset or laughing children during the scan, his brain produces little or no dopamine response. But when he's given brief flashes (each a barely perceptible fraction of a second) of a coke spoon or heroin needle, or images of the old neighborhood in which he used to score drugs, his hippocampus and amygdala light up like a Christmas tree—in spite of his sobriety and what his conscious mind knows about that "old" life, where it led, and what it cost him. The "Go!" system is in charge; the "Stop!" system is mute.

That is what we mean when we say that successful addiction recovery truly involves a rewiring of the brain. With a combination of evidence-based treatments and prescribed medication (when available), it is possible that the brain can recover and undergo the retraining needed to block out the signals that trigger addiction and relearning to respond positively to the experiences that brought happiness before the brain was hijacked by drugs.

7

Alcoholism Is Not a Disease

Jon Burras

Jon Burras, a wellness consultant, is the author of the book Return to Nature: The Five Pillars of Healing *and has written several articles, including "Understanding a Healing Crisis," which can be found on his website,* JonBurras.com.

Programs, treatment centers, and educational resources are part of a multi-billion dollar industry designed to treat alcoholics, an industry that is based on misinformation. The Alcoholics Anonymous movement started it off in the 1930s, claiming that a biological flaw causes alcoholism, and in 1966 the American Medical Association gave further credence to that concept by proclaiming that alcoholism is a disease. The truth is that alcoholism is a choice; there is no genetic dysfunction at its source. And true healing from alcoholism will only come from taking responsibility for bad choices—not from blaming biology.

From backyard barbecues to national holidays, alcohol has become as normal as apple pie and hot dogs. We socialize with alcohol, celebrate with alcohol and medicate with alcohol. While the use of alcohol is normal and embedded in most cultures, there is also a very dark side to this beverage. This dark side has been labeled as "alcoholism."

There is hardly a family that has not been touched by the wrath of alcoholism. From the out-of-control uncle to the mother who partakes in the afternoon while the children are at school, alcoholism has become a normal part of our lives.

From family members to social elites, the scourge of alcoholism has cast its ugly shadow on every corner of our society.

We have developed a multi-billion dollar industry to identify and treat it. There is an abundance of programs available to help control one's drinking. There are Twelve-Step groups, treatment centers and a vast resource of educational books and materials to help contain one's alcoholic tendencies.

Most of what we know about alcoholism is completely false.

Alcoholism Is Not Genetically Induced

Most of us have been led to believe that alcoholism is a genetic inheritance that some people are born with. We are taught that those who have this genetic malady have only one recourse—to never allow alcohol to touch their lips again. They are labeled with the dreaded scarlet letter of being the "alcoholic."

While this way of thinking has become normal in our culture, the irony is that most of what we know about alcoholism is completely false. Alcoholism is not a disease and there is no genetic dysfunction at the source of it all. Most of this story is a "made-up" scientific myth. Here is the truth about alcoholism and all addictions.

Alcohol addiction was the first addiction to be identified and treated because it was the most prevalent and obvious addiction. In the 1930's, Bill Wilson and Dr. Bob [Smith] started the Alcoholics Anonymous movement. This idea was based on the assumption that there was a flaw in some people's biology that made them unable to stop drinking once the first sip of alcohol touched their lips. Despite billions of dollars in scientific research and decades of blaming one's biology, there has never been an alcoholic gene discovered nor has there ever been proven a biological flaw that forced someone to pick up the first drink of alcohol and continue drinking into an out of control state.

In 1960, E. M. Jellinek, a biostatistician at Yale University, published a book called *The Disease Concept of Alcoholism.* Jellinek's initial work consisted of a study of less than 100 men. From these results he concluded that alcoholism was definitely biologically induced. Shortly after, the American Medical Association and American Psychological Association jumped on board and proclaimed that alcoholism was a disease of one's own biology. Western scientific medicine was now the "gate-keeper" of all knowledge in regard to alcoholism and addictions in general.

If one bird flies in the wrong direction then many will follow. Jellinek was the one bird and we have all flown far off course. First off, let's examine the term "alcoholic." The word "alcoholic" is not a scientific term and should not be studied by scientists who pride themselves on measured and quantifiable results. The word "alcoholic" is a subjective term based on who is using it. For instance, magnesium and copper are elements that can be measured and calibrated. Alcoholism cannot be measured. Who is to say that the person who only drinks on weekends is an alcoholic or not? Who is to say that the person who has his two martinis every day at five o'clock is an alcoholic? Who is to say that the person who starts each day with a "Bloody Mary" cocktail and continues to sip alcohol all day long, but never loses control, is an alcoholic or not? You cannot measure "alcoholic." Scientists and medical doctors have been trying to measure every aspect of an alcoholic's biology (genes, proteins, insulin, etc.) for decades now. The problem is that you cannot quantifiably identify who is an alcoholic and who is not because it is not measurable.

Addictions Are Not Diseases

Then let's examine the term "disease." What does it mean to have a disease? Ever since the American Medical Association and scientific medicine came to dominate our lives some one hundred years ago, all disease has been classified as biological in origin. This means that your biology is responsible for how healthy or ill you are. Under this definition, you are not responsible for your health but you can only accept the genes that you were given. Is it any wonder why no auto-immune disease has ever been cured by scientific Western medicine?

All addictions are a choice as a way to medicate yourself from not feeling any uncomfortable feelings.

Disease is a multi-function imbalance. Certainly, if you drank a quart of motor oil your biology will be negatively impacted. But most diseases of our time are not biologically caused. They are based on the thoughts we are thinking, the repression of our emotions and our own stress levels. Alcoholism is no different. Alcoholism is a choice that some people make as a way to mood-alter. That is right! *Alcoholism is a choice; it is not a disease.*

In fact, the knowledge that we have about all addictions stems from the myth that alcoholism is a disease. From gambling addiction to information addiction, petting your dog addiction to surfing the internet addiction, all addictions are a choice as a way to medicate yourself from not feeling any uncomfortable feelings. Just like with alcohol, there has never been found a chocolate addiction gene, a text message addiction gene or even a shopping addiction gene. We know that these addictions exist and they do the same thing to medicate a person from feeling their feelings. A teenager with text message addiction is no different than an out of control alcoholic. Only the means by which one medicates himself tends to be different.

Most of us have never learned how to feel our feelings so we have found ways to mask those feelings. That is what all addictions do—mask feelings. Addictions are a relationship with something that we have chosen to cover up our emotions. An addiction could be a substance (like alcohol), an emotion, a behavior, a thought, a person or an object that is used to hide one's feelings. Nowhere in the equation is there any errant gene, biological allergy or failure of the body.

You might look at addictions as a balancing scale. On one side of the scale are our emotions and on the other side are our addictions. The more one is able to feel his feelings, the less he needs to use an addiction to numb out with. However, the more one chooses not to feel, the more addictions he will have and the stronger those addictions will be.

The problem arises when we look at this old model for healing addictions. We have been stuck on the wrong side of the healing scale. We have been blaming a drug or a substance for our problems. Most have been trying to control the drug or the behavior. We should be working on the other side of the scale learning to feel all the emotions that we have held tightly inside. We have been in a state of blame. Healing happens when we take responsibility and enter into a state of acceptance for the choices we are making. The Western scientific world has a fear of emotions. Scientific medicine derives from the rational brain. The rational brain sees emotions as useless and only for the weak. This is why addictions cannot be healed from the current theory and model. Science is scared of emotions.

Alcoholism Is Emotional—Not Biological

Healing from alcoholism does not come when we substitute one addiction for another—like sobriety. Sobriety is just another term to say that one is now addicted to "control." The addiction pattern continues, only this time the individual gets high from control rather than from being out of control with alcohol. While it may benefit some to learn how to stay in control, this method is not healing and it certainly is not "Recovery." The Recovery Movement has little, if anything, to do with recovery. This method teaches one to be addicted to control. You now use control as your drug of choice.

In fact, this errant scientific biological model has become the foundation for all addictions. From sugar addiction to crystal meth addiction, workaholism to romance addiction, our biology is being blamed for all of it. We remain frozen in place because the original definition of addiction still blames our biology. Healing cannot begin until we go back to the origin and change the definition of addiction. There is an incredible amount of momentum that has been created taking us in the wrong direction because the initial cause has been misdiagnosed.

Healing cannot begin until we go back to the origin and change the definition of addiction.

Healing will happen when you learn how to feel your feelings that you have been fearing. Expression of emotions is the gateway to healing, not attending meetings for life or carrying around the "alcoholic" label forever. Being labeled as "sick" with an "incurable" disease (like alcoholism) is a losing proposition. This is the "victim-conscious" way of seeing the world. Blaming one's biology for the choices that he is making keeps one stuck in place.

There is a solution but it is not to be found at a Twelve-Step meeting or in a scientific laboratory. Healing happens when we begin to follow nature's rhythm and let our emotions out. Alcoholism is not a disease, only a misguided bird flying in the wrong direction. When you begin to change course you will see that healing is as simple as birds flying south in winter (in the Northern Hemisphere) and back north in the summer. Nature is our strongest guide. Follow nature and you will heal; ignore nature and you will suffer.

8

Alcoholism Is a
Genetic Disorder

John Nurnberger, as told to Patrick Perry

John Nurnberger is director of the Institute of Psychiatric Research at Indiana University School of Medicine and a leading researcher on the genetics of alcoholism. Patrick Perry was editor-in-chief of the Saturday Evening Post *for 31 years and is currently director of development and executive editor of The Saturday Evening Post Society.*

Through such studies as the Collaborative Study on the Genetics of Alcoholism, researchers now understand that there is a relationship between genetic factors and alcohol dependence, and are gaining new insight about the specific genes involved and how they work. In fact, such research has shown that fifty percent of alcoholism vulnerability is related to genetic factors. It is important to keep in mind that the way genes behave can be altered and, as a result of this emerging knowledge, effective new treatments and medications are being developed to prevent alcohol abuse.

We've come a long way in understanding the cunning, baffling disease known as alcoholism, and 12-step programs have helped millions of men and women recover.

Historically, alcoholic behavior was blamed on a character flaw or weakness of will. After all, couldn't people stop drink-

John Nurnberger, as told to Patrick Perry (in an interview), "Unraveling the Genetics or Alcoholism: Recent Discoveries Are Paving the Way to Improved Detection, Prevention, and Treatment Strategies for Alcoholism and Other Forms of Substance Abuse," *Saturday Evening Post*, vol. 279, September–October 2007, pp. 50–54. Reproduced by permission.

ing if they really wanted to? While the stigma surrounding alcoholism continues, scientists have gained considerably more insight into how genes and environment interact to affect vulnerability to alcoholism—knowledge that is key to reducing the disease's exacting toll on individuals, families, and society.

As more genes are linked to the development of alcohol dependence and substance abuse, the findings will prove useful in developing tools for better gauging individual risk for the disease and identifying those with alcohol problems. Emerging genetic and environmental insights have also paved the way to the discovery of new therapies targeting specific genes or treatments tailored to individual backgrounds.

The [*Saturday Evening Post*] spoke with John Nurnberger, M.D., Ph.D., director of the Institute of Psychiatric Research at Indiana University School of Medicine and a leading researcher on the genetics of alcoholism for decades.

The Collaborative Study on the Genetics of Alcoholism

Saturday Evening Post: Could you tell us about your work with the Collaborative Study on the Genetics of Alcoholism (COGA), and how alcoholics and family members have helped?

Dr. [John] Nurnberger: COGA is a study that has been continuously supported and funded by the National Institute on Alcohol Abuse and Alcoholism (NIAAA) starting in 1989. Drs. Henri Begleiter from the State University of New York and Ted Reich at Washington University in St. Louis helped launch and direct the initial study, which involved six sites around the country: University of California San Diego, University of Iowa, University of Connecticut, SUNY [State University New York] Downstate Medical Center in Brooklyn, Washington University in St. Louis, and Indiana University in Indianapolis.

For the past 18 years, we have collaborated to identify families through persons diagnosed with alcohol dependence located at treatment facilities. Once we identified the individual, we would obtain permission to contact relatives of the person to discuss diagnoses in the extended family. We would then perform a brain wave study and take blood for DNA analysis.

In this way COGA established a huge database of information on 12,000 persons across the country. We organized the information to illuminate conditions that surfaced in families with a vulnerability to alcohol dependence and also to uncover the relationship of the brain electrical activity and DNA markers to those conditions.

Our group published a number of reports on findings from this sample over the years. We found that a variety of conditions go along with alcohol dependence in families, including dependence on various drugs—marijuana, opiates, tobacco, stimulants, and sedatives. We also noted that a constellation of anxiety and depressive disorders tend to cluster with alcohol problems.

In addition, we observed particular electrical activity signatures in the brain and specific single genes, such as those coding for GABRA2 (a receptor for a transmitter chemical that inhibits other signals), ADH4 (which breaks down alcohol in the body), and CHRM2 (another brain transmitter receptor).

COGA remains very active in various ways: one, we're looking for additional genes in the families we have been studying; and two, we identified adolescents in these families and are following them over time. This is a special high-risk population, and we're trying to determine risk and protective factors that impact young people growing up in families with multiple alcohol-dependent relatives. We are now at a point where some young people in the group are experiencing problems with alcohol but others are not, providing insights into how genes interact with family experience.

In doing the adolescent study, one interesting finding is that the pattern related to specific genes is unexpected. For example, in young people with genetic variations in the GABRA2 neurotransmitter receptor gene, we expected to see alcohol problems and we didn't. Instead, we observed conduct disorder. While you have to study adults to see the alcohol problem, in kids it's more behavior problems. When you look at persons who have the ADH4 gene variant, they begin drinking very early. When you observe persons with the CHRM2 gene variant, they experience depression and anxiety at greater rates as children. Later, they may develop alcohol problems. . . .

Alcoholism has to be thought of as a chronic condition that requires long-term treatment.

New Insights for Treatment

Are 12-step programs like Alcoholics Anonymous still cornerstones of treatment?

Over the years Alcoholics Anonymous [A.A.] has been the most successful single treatment available for alcohol dependence. It still is. The A.A. Twelve Step Program has been adapted for many situations. For example, when adolescents and people with dual diagnoses, such as depression or anxiety, need help with substance abuse problems, A.A. is used. A series of psychotherapies are also under investigation—for example, motivational enhancement.

Alcohol treatment is actually much more successful than people realize. People tend to get a negative picture regarding addiction and the prognosis for people with addiction. It's unwarranted, because many treatments are successful both short- and long-term. People with an effective course of treatment tend to do well for about a year or so initially. A number will then slip back into problems with alcohol, but they seek treatment again, and eventually those who keep trying will be able to maintain their sobriety. Alcoholism has to be thought of as a chronic condition that requires long-term treatment. With that attitude and the ability to support long-term monitoring and treatment, people can recover very successfully from these disorders.

Can someone with a vulnerability to alcoholism also inherit a predisposition to bipolar disorder, depression, or another disorder?

Yes. They both need to be treated. That's been one of the difficulties in the past. In someone with depression and alcohol dependence, if you just treat the depression without the alcohol problem, it won't be effective and vice versa; if you just treat the alcohol problem without thinking about the depression, that's likely also not to be effective. There is an increased risk of alcohol dependence in persons with bipolar illness or depression. About half of people with major depression or bipolar illness will experience problems with alcohol dependence or substance abuse. The risk is about three times over the general population.

Are we at a point where we tailor treatment to best address an individual's specific genetic profile?

Not yet. There are not too many instances in which a genetic test would be of particular value as part of an individual's medical exam for alcohol dependence. But things may change rapidly in the next few years.

Just because a condition is related to genetics doesn't mean it can't be treated or altered.

Genetic Conditions Can Be Treated

In your recent [2007] article in Scientific American, *you wrote, "Genetics is never destiny." What can physicians and members of high-risk families do with the emerging information about vulnerability to alcoholism or substance abuse?*

We are trying to understand the biochemical pathways to vulnerability so that new treatments can be designed. Just because a condition is related to genetics doesn't mean it can't be treated or altered. Genetic vulnerabilities are simply that— vulnerabilities. While you can't alter the DNA code you're born with, you can alter the way the genes are expressed and how your body makes proteins from that DNA. In fact, medications can change gene expression, as can exercise. In effect, you can help turn off or turn on various genes by what you do, what medications you take, and the foods that you eat. It's very important for people to realize that, because there is a prominent notion that "you've got a gene for this or that, therefore the condition is inevitable." That's not at all the case.

We have to think differently about how genes actually work. In the body, gene expression is a very malleable process. We are trying to understand what the specific genes are that relate to alcohol dependence and how they work. We know some of them already, such as the GABRA2, the ADH4, and the CHRM2 that I mentioned. . . .

For alcohol dependence, about 50 percent is related to genetic factors.

Increased Understanding of Genetic Vulnerability

Are we overcoming the stigma associated with these disorders?

Psychiatric illness has been stigmatized. Some think it shameful that people with any disorder might have to see a psychiatrist. There's no reason to think this. The brain is an organ just like the heart. Things go wrong with the brain based on genetics, just like they might go wrong in the heart or liver based on genetics. As we understand more about the treatments people need, the stigma associated with who they are because of genetic vulnerability to anxiety, depression, or addiction will decrease. People will see that no matter what gene variant they were born with (and we all have some), they can do—or not do—things to make life better.

What percentage of vulnerability to alcohol dependence is related to genetics?

For alcohol dependence, about 50 percent is related to genetic factors and the other half to environmental factors, such as availability of alcohol and cultural factors. In comparison, the heritability of bipolar illness is about 80 percent, while the heritability of major depression is about 60 percent. Alcohol dependence is less heritable, but still substantially influenced by genetics. In general, there is rarely a situation where there's a 100 percent chance that someone is going to inherit the disorder, except in a single-gene condition, such as Huntington's disease. Most of the diseases we study and treat are conditions of complex inheritance, where there is an increased or a decreased risk.

What is the clinical difference between alcohol dependence and alcohol abuse?

Alcohol dependence is a more severe condition. We diagnose alcohol abuse if a person has one persistent symptom—driving while intoxicated or using alcohol in a way that it interferes with work or gets a person in trouble socially. If the symptom persists over time, that would be enough for a diagnosis of alcohol abuse.

Persons vulnerable to alcohol dependence have measurable brain differences.

Alcohol dependence, on the other hand, is a more pervasive characteristic. The diagnosis requires three or more symptoms that include loss of control, tolerance and withdrawal, giving up important activities in order to drink, and persistent drinking despite medical consequences. If the problems occur together over the course of a year or longer, we would call that alcohol dependence.

Are brain electrical activity patterns different between alcoholics and nonalcoholics? If so, could we include an EEG [electroencephalogram] as a useful clinical tool in the diagnosis of alcoholism?

We use the electrical activity of the brain to provide information for research purposes, but not really for clinical purposes. Brain imaging could at some point be used for clinical purposes. But we are primarily trying to understand whether there is a difference in the electrical activity of the brain in persons vulnerable to alcohol dependence. We studied persons with alcohol problems and their relatives—those who drank and those who didn't. We found consistent differences in attention, response to stimuli like sounds and lights, and the predominant frequency of brain wave activity. It appears that persons vulnerable to alcohol dependence have measurable brain differences in terms of the electrical activity. For one, there appeared to be decreased attention to important stimuli in persons vulnerable to alcohol dependence. It also appeared as though there was decreased evidence of inhibition in the cortex area of the brain, which could be related to increased impulsivity. We believe it relates to the activity of GABA [gamma-Aminobutyric acid], a major inhibitory neurotransmitter in the brain. Like many of our findings, the hope is that these observations may one day translate into a target for intervention.

In studies of children of alcoholics who were adopted by nondrinking families, does alcohol tend to emerge less often, harking back to the role of the environment?

While we haven't done adoption studies in Indiana, studies have been done, primarily in Scandinavian countries that have central records of adoption and psychiatric hospitalization that investigators can access. It does appear that the chance for alcohol dependence is greater in adopted-away children of alcoholics, even if they are not brought up in families with the alcoholic person. One still faces increased risk from the genes.

What is your overall hope by identifying genetic influences on vulnerability?

Identifying genetic influences helps us on the road to self-knowledge and leads to strategies for optimal health and a productive life. The field is opening up in front of us. We will witness very real changes in the next couple of decades.

9

Alcoholics Anonymous Is an Effective Treatment Program

A.J. Adams

A.J. Adams, a recovering alcoholic, is a professional writer, consultant, and teacher. A.J. Adams is a pen name.

Someone once called the Alcoholics Anonymous program "the adjustable wrench that fits any nut," an apt description for afflicted individuals who cobble together their own unique recovery with the guidance tool of the Twelve Steps. By recognizing that the disease of alcoholism has physical, mental, and spiritual components, the founders of Alcoholics Anonymous created an enduring treatment program that has proven successful in treating two million cases of alcoholism.

Alcoholism has been wrecking lives and killing people for thousands of years. It's strange to think that so little was known about it until fairly recently, especially when you consider how many people have been damaged over the millennia. To be fair, you could probably say the same thing about heart disease, diabetes, or cancer. But what's different about alcoholism is its most effective twenty-first century treatment modality is a lay fellowship founded by nonexperts early in the last century that does not rely on medications or medical procedures. While insulin, radiation, statins, antibiotics, chemotherapy, and other high-tech remedies have been marshaled against all the other major diseases, alcoholism is still most successfully treated in a nineteenth-century revival-tent support-group mode. Does anyone else think this is odd?

A.J. Adams, *Undrunk: A Skeptic's Guide to AA*, Center City, MN: Hazelden, 2009, pp. 27–30, 42–46, 50, 62. Copyright © 2009 by A. J. Adams. Reproduced by permission.

You'll hear over and over in AA [Alcoholics Anonymous] that there's no use questioning how the program works. As if to settle the matter once and for all, AAs everywhere chant at the end of each meeting: "It works if you work it." When I was a newcomer, that sounded ridiculous to me. But as the days and months went by, I started to wonder whether trying to figure out AA was a waste of time. I was continually amazed at what AA gave me on a daily basis—clearly, my long-term life prospects were improving miraculously. AA was not unlike the watch I could not possibly build but that always told me exactly what time it was. Or, as a friend of mine calls AA, "the adjustable wrench that fits any nut."

But since I'm an alcoholic, I want to know things for myself. So I tried to unwrap, unwind, and understand the inner workings and hidden mechanisms of AA. Here's what I found.

The early AAs recognized that alcoholism had physical, mental, and spiritual components.

Early Alcoholics Anonymous

I tried to imagine what it must have been like sitting around with the first AA groups in Akron or New York in the early 1930s. To a man (they were all men), they had been given up for dead by medicine. Each entered AA dry, but many couldn't stay that way and left. The ones who stayed seemed to know that sticking together somehow helped them stay sober. They sensed that there was a physical aspect to their alcoholism, and a few doctors were beginning to support that. But no one knew what the pathology was, much less how to treat it. Eventually, as they exchanged stories and experiences, they realized that they had partly thought their way into alcoholism. Maybe they could think their way out of it.

None of these insights qualified as a breakthrough on its own, but taken together, they were interesting. When these early AAs added spirituality to the mix, they started thinking in terms of treatment. If the alcohol craving was physical and an alcoholic could not reason it away, the only hope for these men was spiritual. At that time, there was a fair amount of popular psychology around promoting various mind-over-matter therapies, for example, New Thought, Positive Thinking, and Mary Baker Eddy's Christian Science. Each emphasized "letting go" or "surrender" to a higher power. At the same time, religious organizations like the Oxford Group were trying out spiritual remedies on drunks with some success. The spiritual principles behind these remedies probably influenced the design of the Twelve Steps. Finally, tent-show revivals across rural America were also flogging spiritual cures.

As the early AAs recognized that alcoholism had physical, mental, and spiritual components, the outline of a three-pronged treatment approach was coming into sight. The spiritual component catalyzed the other two, setting AA in motion and setting it apart from all other approaches. The early AA groups were different from what we think of today as support groups. The members were not only there to commiserate with each other but were also determined to find a remedy for their disease before they died of it. With that incentive, the early AAs identified three components of a possible treatment approach as they essentially talked their way through the problem.

The Twelve Step AA program is a treatment modality that is still in use, with proven success in 2 million cases of alcoholism.

First, they thought of alcoholism as a uniquely personal disease. All illnesses affect individual persons, but only alcoholism could actually be treated by the afflicted person—and *only* by that person. This kind of challenge appealed to the pioneer spirit in Bill and Bob [co-founders of AA, Bill Wilson and Bob Smith]. Second, they had to reconcile this individual challenge with their certainty that recovery could not occur in solitude. A group process was crucial. This required teamwork. Finally, Bill and Bob knew they had to pass on the AA message to ensure their own sobriety and the survival of the fellowship. A spirit of community led AA outside its tight-knit groups to alcoholics who still suffered. The publishing of the *Big Book* in 1939 took the message national and, eventually, global.

Think about this: A hundred regular Joes with a common fatal and incurable illness got together and decided that they were suffering in body, mind, and spirit. Their new concept of alcoholism was a medical breakthrough. They decided that they would treat themselves in a group setting on the basis of a dozen rules one of them thought up. The Twelve Step AA program is a treatment modality that is still in use, with proven success in 2 million cases of alcoholism. The early AAs applied three American civic virtues to do the job: pioneer spirit, team spirit, and community spirit. Pretty amazing. . . .

Spirituality Is the Key to Success

It's hard to describe how adding a spiritual dimension to my life makes me feel. Anything I say is bound to sound corny, naive, and maybe even made up. But 2 million other AAs are getting something spiritual out of the program too, and we can't all be wrong about this. So, here goes.

In AA, spirituality is its own reward.

I can think of four tangible benefits of opening up to the spirituality that seems to be a natural result of working the Steps. First, the obsession and craving for alcohol left me. I never thought this would be possible. I believe it's a daily reprieve, but I have a little more confidence in it with every day that goes by. Second, I'm not so damn worried about everything. The fear and anxiety that were my constant companions as a drinker have largely been replaced by assurance and optimism. Not everything is settled in my personal affairs, nor is it ever likely to be. But I seem to know what to work on and how. I'm generally confident that things will turn out, and most things do. Third, I feel as though I've been let in on a few things that previously eluded me, such as these: What's really important? Who am I and what am I supposed to be doing? How do I make things better for me, mine, and others? Finally, I see the day-to-day world in a noticeably different way. My natural surroundings are more beautiful. People I meet are nicer and more interesting. Books I read seem to have more significance. I have new solutions for old problems, and not as many new problems. I'm happier, and I look forward to the routine and the surprises of daily life.

In AA, spirituality is its own reward. It is the source of energy to face my life with confidence. Rationalism, science, and all the other stuff in the reality family couldn't help me with my alcoholic despair because they exclude the personal and the private. Spirituality was the missing piece for me. I don't really know how spirituality works. For now, I've concluded that it's not knowable, only doable. Because I have to see and touch things to believe them, spirituality had to yield results for me in every important part of my life: family, job, friends, dreams, and aspirations. It has.

I don't worry about losing my shiny new spirituality. I assume I have it to use it. As long as my spiritual side gets regular exercise, I'll be okay. We alcoholics are happiest and most successful when we regularly do the right thing in three areas of our lives: for ourselves and our sobriety, for other alcoholics, and for everyone else. Simple, really. . . .

Some AA Basics

AA's philosophy and program will not dazzle you in the same way that the general theory of relativity might. But, as a combination of intellectual simplicity and spiritual depth, AA sets the gold standard. The program is laid out in the first 164 pages of the *Big Book* in simple declarative sentences, with helpful examples and an endearing earnestness. Intellectual gymnastics and academic showing off are nowhere to be found in the *Big Book*. Bill Wilson wrote the AA message on the basis of a solid liberal arts education, using a no-frills writing style and relying on the unvarnished group experience of the original AA members.

So where does the depth come from? I believe that the AA philosophy is profound, in part, because of what each person reads into it. We get some fairly clear and concise guidance on what to do. The Twelve Steps, for instance, are concisely worded and conveniently numbered. But each of us must decide how we feel about them and what they mean. This customizing option of the AA program is its true genius, in my view. Each person cobbles together a unique recovery. We try out different approaches with our sponsors and groups. In the end, if it works, it's the right answer. If not, we keep tinkering. This appealed to me, and I think it appeals to many other independent-minded AAs. . . .

How important is the AA meeting in the greater scheme of things? I believe it's the soul of AA. It's where the message is shared. It is a reservoir of experience, strength, and hope for newcomers and oldtimers alike. The meeting is the face of AA to thousands of people who are looking for something that they can't quite put their finger on. It's the core institution of the AA community for those of us who are already members. This loose collection of more than 100,000 quasi-independent groups, meeting in locations around the globe, is the solid foundation of the largest single fellowship in the world. AAs on oil rigs can participate in meetings via e-mail, and our magazine, the *AA Grapevine*, is referred to as a "meeting in print." The group ensures AA unity through its independence. We recover by helping others to recover. Much of this occurs at meetings. . . .

Progress, Not Perfection

I've never heard anyone say, "I plan to stay in AA forever." Just as our reprieve from the alcohol craving is a daily event, our membership in AA renews every twenty-four hours. It's not unusual for people to stop coming to meetings for a while or for good. Sometimes they fall victim to complacency and old thinking; sometimes after years of sobriety, they feel sure that they're cured and it's okay to rejoin the party. The best way to avoid "going out" is to know where AA is taking us and to enjoy the journey. "Progress, not perfection" is AA's Global Positioning System. This is how it works.

Of the Twelve Steps, only one—the first one—needs to be taken perfectly and fully: *We admitted we were powerless over alcohol—that our lives had become unmanageable.* The other eleven Steps set out ideals toward which we work. No AA is expected to fully execute those eleven Steps. Honest effort and solid progress are enough to secure our sobriety and good standing with our Higher Power and our fellows. As long as we're making progress, we're making the grade in AA.

10

Alcoholics Anonymous Is a Flawed Treatment Program

Cynthia Perkins

Cynthia Perkins, a mental health professional and a recovered alcoholic and drug addict, holds a bachelor's degree in psychology and a master's degree in counseling. She is the author of several self-help books, including Get Sober Stay Sober: The Truth About Alcoholism *and* Living Life to the Fullest: Creative Coping Strategies for Living with Chronic Illness.

Alcoholics Anonymous is an incomplete treatment program with a low success rate because it ignores the biochemical roots of alcoholism. Medical research and scientific evidence have shown that alcoholism has its roots in malfunctioning or depleted neurotransmitters in the brain. To be successful, therefore, a treatment program for alcohol abuse must restore a balance to neurotransmitters and body chemistry, which can be achieved through diet, environment, and nutritional supplementation. Alcoholics Anonymous and other twelve-step programs are outdated and insufficient because they do not address these biochemical factors. In fact, studies have shown their success rates to be as low as .01 percent for over five years of sobriety, while treatment centers that focus on biochemistry report a success rate as high as eighty-four percent.

There are several flaws or problems with Alcoholics Anonymous. First and foremost is that it is an incomplete ap-

Cynthia Perkins, M.Ed., "The Problem with Alcoholics Anonymous," www.Alternatives-for-Alcoholism.com, 2009. Reproduced by permission of the author.

proach to alcoholism. There is no denying that it does have many good benefits that are helpful to some people, but it is limited to a select few.

It offers emotional support, people you can relate to, a place to go to fill your time and feel connected to others, helps you reconnect with your morals and values which have most often been obliterated by drunkenness, helps break down denial, build a new social life that takes you away from the old places and friends, educates, provides structure and hope and gives people something to hang onto. These are all great aspects, but it does not encompass all that is needed.

Spirituality Alone Does Not Cure

Nourishing a rich spiritual life is an important component of maintaining long-term sobriety, but it is not the only component and it's not always essential. People who don't believe in God or follow a spiritual path can still find sobriety by addressing their biochemical issues. Not only that, it does not address the biochemical root of alcoholism, which is why relapse is so common.

The other point of issue with the spiritual/religious aspect in Alcoholics Anonymous, is that AA comes very close to being its own religion. It tends to be a little punitive, rigid and shaming and tries to brainwash the individual into believing everything they say is true and abiding by their rules. It encourages powerlessness, which can be counterproductive. Regardless of how defiantly they deny it, AA is a religious program.

Spirituality is about the relationship you have with your core self and the world around you and finding meaning and purpose in your life, while religion is about beliefs and practices that involve God or a higher power. AA and the 12 steps clearly fall under the religion category.

Spirituality is a very personal, individualized experience. People get very mixed up and think of religion and spirituality as one. Being spiritual does not necessarily have anything to do with religion or God, although religion tries to make you believe they are one in the same.

Not many people can make a full recovery with spirituality alone because the real cause of addiction is not addressed.

I don't believe in a "higher power" and yet consider myself a deeply spiritual person. My spiritual connection and fulfillment is found in nature, meditation, writing and my relationship with self and others.

Living a spiritual life does not have to include a relationship with a higher power and one does not have to embrace the whole powerlessness concept. We are not powerless over addiction. If the alcoholic addresses the biochemical roots of their alcoholism, they are empowered to take control of their recovery path.

There is nothing fundamentally wrong with using spirituality to assist in recovery of any illness, as a matter of fact, it is an essential component of my life, but not many people can make a full recovery with spirituality alone because the real cause of addiction is not addressed. Additionally, not everyone can embrace this concept. Many people with alcoholism are too damaged physically and emotionally to begin working on their spiritual life, and some people are uncomfortable with the whole spiritual/religious aspect of AA, and other people don't believe in God.

Even those individuals who already have strong religious or spiritual beliefs most often do not succeed in long-term sobriety, which leads us to the most important flaw in Alcoholics Anonymous.

Alcoholics Anonymous Programs
Have Low Success Rates

The biggest problem with Alcoholics Anonymous is that it has a very low success rate for long term sobriety. Accurate statistics are hard to come by because of many factors, such as anonymity and dishonesty, but most studies reveal that it only has about a 2.5 percent success rate for over 5 years of sobriety. Some statistics have it as low as .01 percent.

Those who do recover using a 12 step program fight constant cravings to drink and suffer with a variety of other symptoms.

Putting all statistics aside, one only needs to ask around any Alcoholics Anonymous meeting to clearly see what the statistics are. At any given meeting at any given time most people that are present are newcomers. Membership usually consists of people who have only a day sober or a few days or weeks. There are a few people who have 90 days or 120 and maybe 1 or 2 people with 6 months or one year. Depending on the size of the meeting, there may be one, or if you're really lucky two old timers, someone with more than 5 years. Old timers are far and few between.

Most alcoholics do not recover from their disease, they die. Those who do recover using a 12 step program fight constant cravings to drink and suffer with a variety of other symptoms like irritability, anxiety, tension, fatigue and depression that has a deep impact on the quality of their life and forces them to be dependent upon attending Alcoholics Anonymous (AA) meetings the rest of their life.

Staying sober is a constant battle and they continue to be addicted to a variety of other substances and activities like sugar, caffeine, sex and cigarettes. Even Bill Wilson (aka Bill W.), the founder of Alcoholics Anonymous, was plagued with symptoms like depression and fatigue and remained an incurable addict in more ways than one until the day he died. It is not well known information, but the infamous Bill Wilson was severely addicted to nicotine, caffeine and sex. His, so called divinely guided messages from God, were actually the result of hallucinations, sexual obsession and shame.

Additionally, we're talking about long-term sobriety, not short-term. Sure, a good deal of people can get a few months of sobriety or a year under their belt with some serious white knuckling, but in the overall picture of life, one year is not a long time. That does not constitute long-term, stable sobriety. Not only that, continuously fighting overwhelming cravings to drink does not constitute success.

Regardless of how defiantly AA denies it, the bottom line is that AA and all 12 step programs are religious programs that employ the use of a variety of cult-like practices that drive many people out the door and back to the bottle.

Another important fact to keep in mind is that almost all alcoholism treatment centers are based on the 12 step program and demand that all patients attend Alcoholics Anonymous. AA meetings are built into the treatment curriculum and the 12 steps and serenity prayer are recited several times a day. So that means that treatment centers are having about the same success rate and failures as AA. Alcoholics Anonymous and traditional treatment are basically one in the same.

When I was in rehab 21 years ago, our counselor told us that only 3 of us would still be around in a year. There were approximately 30 of us in rehab at the time. I remember feeling horrified by that number, but I was determined I would be one of those three.

Experts report that spontaneous remission of alcoholism will occur about .05 percent of the time, so you actually have a better chance of staying sober without treatment and alcoholics anonymous.

Another problem with Alcoholics Anonymous is that it promotes dependence on the program. It replaces one addiction with another, instead of teaching the individual how to take the skills they learn and apply them to their life outside the program. They will brain wash you into believing you must attend Alcoholics Anonymous meetings for the rest of your life or you'll get drunk. This simply is not true. Once you address the biochemical issues of alcoholism, staying sober is no longer an issue. Alcoholics Anonymous should be a transitional phase for the early phases of recovery, not something you're sentenced to for the rest of your life. . . .

AA and 12 step treatment programs refuse to even look at new scientific evidence . . . and continue to treat addiction with an outdated model.

Treatment Programs Should Accommodate New Scientific Information

What is it that Alcoholics Anonymous and traditional rehabilitation is missing?

Alcoholics Anonymous was formally developed in 1935. Since that time we have learned an astounding amount of information and have a much better understanding of the addiction process. Scientific evidence now tells us that alcoholism, or any addiction, has its roots in malfunctioning, imbalanced or depleted neurotransmitters in the brain, nutritional deficiencies and allergy. Yet AA and 12 step programs have not grown or expanded their treatment approach in any way. With all other physical diseases, we consistently update and change our treatment approaches as we learn more information about the terrain; but that is not the case with alcoholism or addiction, it remains stubbornly stuck in the past.

AA and 12 step treatment programs refuse to even look at new scientific evidence, listen to new insights or hear anything that contradicts the original AA principles, and continue to treat addiction with an outdated model that besides being sexist, shaming, abusive, cult like and patriarchal isn't and never has been very successful. What's even worse is that they rationalize and justify their failure by blaming the victim.

Alcoholics Anonymous and the 12 steps are based on the beliefs of a Christian evangelical cult called the Oxford Group that attempts to control people's behavior through guilt, mind control and shaming them into submission rather than a real medical treatment that focuses on the true physiological roots of alcoholism. These distasteful practices have resulted in the largest part of the addicted population to fail to maintain sobriety and/or take issue with the current treatment approach and often walk away.

Most people do not succeed in a 12 step program because it is an ineffective program that does not address the true root of alcoholism, but AA does not consider that as a failure of the program. Instead they blame the alcoholic with statements like "they haven't hit their bottom yet," "they're in denial," or "they didn't work the program." When in reality, that has nothing to do with it.

> For successful recovery from alcoholism . . . there must be biochemical repairs.

People leave or don't succeed with AA and 12 step treatment programs for a variety of very valid and healthy reasons such as they are uncomfortable with: the powerlessness concept; the "group think" mentality; the religious aspect; the abusive aspect; the rigid, dogmatic structure; the shaming; the blaming; the sexist aspect; the patriarchal aspect; the archaic aspect; the demeaning aspect; the abusive criticizing on the hot seat; and the cult-like brainwashing methods to name a few. Then since there are no other treatment options available to them, they return to drinking.

Biochemical Repairs Are Needed

People do not succeed with AA and the 12 step program because it does not address the true root of alcoholism. For successful recovery from alcoholism and long term sobriety without intense cravings and discomfort there must be biochemical repairs.

Biochemical repairs consist of restoring balance to the neurotransmitters and body chemistry through diet, environment and nutritional supplementation. Conditions like food allergies or sensitivities, hypoglycemia, hypothyroidism, candida overgrowth, chemical sensitivities and nutritional deficiencies, which alter neurotransmitters need to be addressed.

The alcoholic cannot continue to smoke, eat sugar, drink coffee and eat grains because they keep the addiction process active. They must stabilize their blood sugar and make major life style changes.

When I began to make biochemical repairs, all the symptoms that had plagued me for most of my life and led to my drinking disappeared. The depression, anxiety, irritability, cravings to drink or drug etc. etc. were all miraculously gone. . . .

Cravings to drink *did not* return. As a matter of fact, drinking was no longer an issue at all in my life. I didn't think about it or struggle with it, period.

It's been over 20 years now and I continue to be sober without cravings. I haven't attended a meeting in about 18 years. I went back to college and picked up a couple degrees in psychology and counseling and now dedicate my life to educating anyone who will listen about the importance of biochemical issues in regard to addiction and mental health.

Alternative treatment centers that approach alcoholism from a biochemical viewpoint, as I have described above, have a success rate of about 75 percent and even as high as 84 percent. . . .

I'm ... not here to try and convince anyone not to attend AA. As I mentioned earlier, there are definite benefits to the 12 step program, especially in the early phases of recovery, and if you're one of those people who find Alcoholics Anonymous to be a good fit, but still can't achieve sobriety, then perhaps you need a combination of both.

As the saying goes, "Take what works and leave the rest."

I am here to provide the alcoholic with the facts so they can make the choice that is best for them.

If traditional treatment centers incorporated biochemical repairs into their program along with Alcoholics Anonymous, we could see amazing results.

11

Cognitive Therapy Can Be an Effective Treatment for Alcoholism

Ann M. Manzardo, Donald W. Goodwin, Jan L. Campbell, Elizabeth C. Penick, and William F. Gabrielli

Ann M. Manzardo is assistant professor and pharmacologist in the Department of Psychiatry and Behavioral Science; Donald W. Goodwin was a University Distinguished Professor, Emeritus; Jan L. Campbell is a professor of psychiatry and director of the Addiction Psychiatry Fellowship Program, Department of Psychiatry and Behavioral Sciences; Elizabeth C. Penick is professor and director, Division of Psychology, Department of Psychiatry and Behavioral Sciences; and William F. Gabrielli is professor of psychiatry and internal medicine and chairman of the Department of Psychiatry and Behavioral Sciences; all at the University of Kansas Medical Center.

Cognitive therapy has become an increasingly popular and successful way to treat alcohol addiction. In cognitive therapy, the patient learns how to identify thoughts that trigger drinking, and then to substitute more positive and constructive thoughts aimed at producing a healthier lifestyle. Furthermore, cognitive therapy for alcoholics—which can be given to individuals or groups, involves a brief amount of time, and is relatively inexpensive—has been shown by many studies to be just as effective as longer and more expensive inpatient programs.

Ann M. Manzardo, Donald W. Goodwin, Jan L. Campbell, Elizabeth C. Penick, and William F. Gabrielli Jr., *Alcoholism: The Facts*, Oxford: Oxford University Press, 2008, pp. 118–121. Copyright © Oxford University Press 2008. Reproduced by permission of Oxford University Press.

'Cognitive' means to learn or know. In recent years, several new 'cognitive' approaches to the treatment of alcoholism have been proposed. They are called by a variety of names but have two elements in common: they are brief, and they involve trying to change a patient's way of thinking.

The 'disease' model compares the alcoholic with a rider who may believe that he can control his horse, but this is an illusion. The horse is the master. All the rider can do is get off—give up alcohol. Not so, says the cognitive therapist. The patient can guide the horse. He can change his drinking behavior by changing his thoughts. Here are some approaches to thought management and the names that they go by.

Changing a Person's Way of Thinking

Cognitive-behavior therapy has a general goal and specific technique for controlling harmful drinking. The word behavior simply refers to the way people behave—not conditioning. Looking for a better treatment for depression, the American psychiatrist Aaron Beck found that depressed people stopped being depressed if they stopped having depressing thoughts. Although this sounds easier said than done, he insisted that depressed patients did not have to have depressed thoughts and that he could help them to have undepressed thoughts. He developed a rather simple set of techniques for doing this, and cognitive therapy became widely popular for almost every known psychiatric condition, including alcoholism.

In the case of depression, studies show that cognitive therapy is sometimes as good as drugs and that a combination of cognitive therapy and drugs sometimes produces the best results of all. Evidence that it is effective for the addictions, including alcoholism, has been mixed, with some studies showing that it helps and others showing that it does not. In any case, cognitive therapy for alcoholism, going under several names, has been the most studied of all alcoholism treatments and has the advantage of being brief and therefore cost-effective. Long and expensive inpatient programs for alcoholics (often following the Minnesota Plan) have been shown in many studies to be no more effective than brief and relatively inexpensive outpatient treatment. The latter usually consists of giving advice and sometimes performing cognitive therapy, as well as encouraging the patient to attend Alcoholics Anonymous, at least in the USA.

Cognitive therapy . . . often begins with attempts to help the patient identify thought patterns that undermine self-esteem and engender anxiety.

Identifying Undermining Thoughts

Cognitive therapy aimed at changing a person's behavior (which is why it is called cognitive-behavior therapy) often begins with attempts to help the patient identify thought patterns that undermine self-esteem and engender anxiety. The therapist teaches the patient how to identify negative assumptions that the patient makes about self and others, and suggests ways to reframe problems and behaviors more realistically. To some extent this is based on the assumption that people cannot have two opposing thoughts simultaneously. One cannot think, 'I am miserable and therefore must drink' and simultaneously think 'I'm feeling pretty good, so why should I drink?' Instead the person should say, 'I am a unique individual. Just because I am the son of my father does not mean I should behave like my father'. The therapist points out 'errors of logic' that the patient can correct if he perceives the errors to be errors and practices thinking good thoughts about himself. The practice takes the form of self-statements, another way of saying that the patient must learn to talk to himself. He should avoid talking to himself out loud in public— those around might misunderstand—but by suspending the use of his vocal cords a person can carry on a conversation with himself without seeming psychotic. In privacy, speaking one's own thoughts aloud can sometimes reveal errors in thinking, similar to trying to explain a thought to another person. Verbalizing a thought often exposes unrecognized assumptions that may be inaccurate.

After several sessions with a cognitive therapist the patient has usually acquired a collection of self-statements, sometimes called 'bumper stickers'. Common ones include, 'There is only today' and 'All of us will be dead in 100 years'. (The latter sounds depressing but actually can be reassuring if the person worries overly about how others view him.) A favorite bumper sticker comes from William James: 'Wisdom is about learning what to overlook'. This covers a whole range of irritations at home, at work, and driving in heavy traffic.

These are self-statements intended to help patients think better of themselves (and probably, by extension, think better of others). Presumably, it would help anybody who 'automatically' reacts negatively to everything and everybody around them, often including the therapist. Thinking, it turns out, need not be entirely automatic. The thinker need not be entirely a passive victim of his thoughts. Patients are sometimes amazed to learn how easily they can substitute constructive healthy thoughts for gloomy thoughts. Probably some people possess the skill more than others (maybe because of genes), and, like all arts, the art of positive thinking requires effort and concentration. The experienced cognitive therapist can help even those congenital 'awfulizers' from interpreting whatever happens to them as awful.

Practicing New Behavior

Cognitive therapy is more active than many talk therapies because it requires that the alcoholic learn and rehearse new responses to new thinking patterns, identify and practice different coping behaviors, learn new social skills and apply those skills in sessions, learn how to monitor moods and respond to unanticipated mood changes, and plan and implement lifestyle changes. It is not enough to talk about feelings; the alcoholic must practice the new behavior until the behavior becomes comfortable. One form of cognitive-behavior therapy called 'dialectical behavior therapy' emphasizes learning new skills of interpreting other people's behavior, deciding how to respond, and developing specific scripts and scenarios

One reason alcoholics feel hopeless about their drinking is that they painfully remember all the times they managed to abstain entirely or moderate their intake only to go back to heavy drinking. The serious form of alcohol dependence called alcoholism is, by most definitions, a chronic condition characterized by frequent relapse. *Relapse prevention* is a name for one form of cognitive therapy. It involves identifying 'high-risk' situations associated with relapse. This may differ from drinker to drinker, but common high-risk situations include parties, celebrations, holiday, hunger, fatigue, and loneliness. When situations most likely to produce relapse are identified in a particular patient, coping skills are then imparted for dealing with the situations. This may involve avoiding parties or, on the contrary, learning new social skills so the person can feel comfortable at the party while nursing an orange juice.

Much depends on whether the alcoholic is 'prepared' to stop drinking.

Some therapists believe that this can be achieved by a sheer act of will. Others disagree and point out that many aspects of a person's social life may not be manipulable in the office of a therapist and may be crucial in determining whether the person relapses. These critics view alcohol consumption as a social behavior driven by social forces. Relapse is believed to represent a response to social pressures such as unemployment, marital conflict, social isolation, and peer influence. The changes that the patient needs in order to avoid relapse do not occur entirely within the person. The therapist should help find him a job, conduct marriage counseling, and help him find a friend or hobby. This may involve increasing the drinker's job-finding skills, or getting him a driver's license, and taking out a newspaper subscription. This is sometimes called community reinforcement. It requires a lot of time and effort on the part of the therapist, more than most therapists are able to provide even if inclined to do so.

Practitioners of relapse prevention do not always strive to keep the patient (or client as he is often called) from drinking entirely. Moderation may be the goal, particularly for patients with mild forms of alcohol dependence. Of course, relapse prevention in the severely alcoholic person is more difficult to achieve, and most agree that much depends on whether the alcoholic is 'prepared' to stop drinking. This is based on the observation that people seem to stop drinking when they are ready to do so, and if they are not ready then professional intervention is of little help.

Carlo DiClemente and William Miller, psychologists who have studied psychotherapy for alcoholics for many years, have proposed that when therapy is not useful, it may be that the therapist needs to see the problem from the same perspective as the alcoholic. In this way of thinking, behavior change occurs in evolving stages, and motivation to change is dependent on the stage the alcoholic has reached. For example, if the alcoholic is beginning to think about getting sober because he was convicted of driving under the influence, the therapist might focus on how treatment and sobriety could influence legal consequences. The therapist's job is to identify the motivational factors for the alcoholic, and direct the therapy so that the alcoholic can use that motivation to reach his goals. It is usually evident that drinking is blocking ways of reaching goals, and sometimes the alcoholic can forgo drinking because the motivation to reach another goal is sufficiently strong and the goal appears feasible.

Cognitive-behavioral therapy goes by many names: CBT, relapse prevention training, social skills training, behavior self-control training, stress management, and others. They can all be given as individual therapy or in groups, and all involve changing a person's way of thinking. They have the advantage of being cost-effective, and have a more substantial database supporting reduction of alcoholic drinking and improving some aspects of quality of life.

12

Binge Drinking Is a Serious Problem for Underage Drinkers

Emily Listfield

Emily Listfield is a former magazine editor-in-chief and author of five novels. Her writing has appeared in the New York Times, Harper's Bazaar, Redbook, Self, Ladies' Home Journal, New York Magazine, Parade, *and many other publications.*

It is not uncommon for college students to drink alcohol; even high school and middle school students have been known to sneak drinks. But binge drinking—defined as men drinking at least five alcoholic beverages or women drinking four within two hours—is becoming increasingly widespread among teenagers and is causing major concern for parents, physicians, school campus officials, and alcohol-related experts. Because their goal is to get drunk as quickly as possible, teenagers mix alcohol with super-caffeinated energy drinks or imbibe massive amounts of "user friendly" flavored drinks that have a high alcohol content. As a result, hospital emergency rooms are seeing more and more youths with blood alcohol levels four to five times the legal limit for driving, which can have fatal consequences.

Linda B. and her husband were sound asleep when the phone rang at 2 a.m. Their oldest daughter, Rory, 18, had left two weeks earlier for her first year at a college in Connecticut. An honor student and athlete, Rory had never been in trouble. They didn't think they had any reason to worry. "When I picked up the phone, Rory was crying hysterically; she was completely disoriented," Linda recalls. "She kept saying, 'Mom, can you come get me?' but she had no idea where she was—and we live hours away. I've never been that scared—she could barely speak." Finally, Linda heard other people's voices in the background and had Rory pass the phone to someone who told her where they were. While Linda stayed on the line with her daughter, her husband called campus security. When officials found Rory a few minutes later, her face was covered in blood. She had fallen and broken her nose, though she was so intoxicated that she hadn't realized it. "She managed to tell me she'd been drinking something called Jungle Juice," Linda recalls.

For many teens, the point is to get as drunk as possible, as quickly and cheaply as possible.

Extreme Drinking

Like many parents, Linda had never heard of the potentially lethal concoction. A syrupy mix of hard liquors and fruit juices, it often includes Everclear, whose alcohol content can be as high as 190 proof (a level banned in some states). Some kids throw in energy drinks for good measure. There are dozens of recipes for Jungle Juice online; one popular site calls it "Suicide in a Kettle."

Kegs and watered-down beer have long been as much a part of the campus experience as trying to avoid early-morning classes. And it's not exactly unheard of for teens in high school and even middle school to sneak into their parents' liquor cabinets. What is new—and increasingly alarming to those confronting the issue—is the rising trend of extreme underage drinking. Such is the concern that the legal drinking age itself has come into question. Some argue that lowering it from 21 to 18 would help curb the behavior by de-mystifying alcohol. Critics point out that drunk-driving fatalities among teens have dropped greatly since the drinking age became 21 nationwide. But both sides agree that binge drinking is a growing problem.

"We're seeing kids coming in with blood alcohol levels in the mid-.3s, even .4, which is four to five times the legal limit for driving. That's the level at which 50% of people die," says Dr. Mary Claire O'Brien, an emergency medicine physician and assistant professor at Wake Forest University School of Medicine in North Carolina who specializes in alcohol-related research. "Ten years ago, we saw those levels only in chronic alcoholics."

Adolescents tend to drink differently than adults. Their goal is not to sit around enjoying a glass or two of wine over the course of an evening. Rather, for many teens, the point is to get as drunk as possible, as quickly and cheaply as possible, in part to reduce the social anxiety rife at that age. Unfortunately, there are now more—and more dangerous—ways to accomplish this than ever before. The practice of mixing alcohol with super-caffeinated energy drinks; the marketing of flavored malt beverages in 23.5-ounce cans, each containing a serious dose of alcohol; a shift in preference from beer to hard liquor; and the influence of social media, through which kids avidly share Jungle Juice recipes and tales of their exploits, have all raised the stakes.

If you think your kids are immune, think again. According to the CDC [Center for Disease Control and Prevention], about 90% of all teen alcohol consumption occurs in the form of binge drinking, which, experts say, peaks at age 19. Forty-one percent of 12th graders report having had a drink in the previous 30 days, and by the time kids are in college, that number climbs to 72%. Approximately 200,000 adolescents visit emergency rooms each year because of drinking-related incidents, and more than 1,700 college students die.

"Underage drinking doesn't discriminate," says Adrian Lopez, director of community outreach for the SoBeSober program for teens in Miami. "Whether you are an upper-middle-class, straight-A student or from an inner city, it impacts all demographics and communities. And it often peaks in May and June, when kids are celebrating proms and graduations. We call it 'The Killing Season.'"

"Blackout in a Can"

The craze for combining energy drinks, which can have far more caffeine than coffee or cola, with alcohol is particularly troubling. Dr. O'Brien first became aware of the phenomenon in 2006 when a student was brought in near-comatose. "The caffeine blocks the part of alcohol that makes you sleepy and might otherwise cause you to pass out. This enables you to drink far more than you might have. By the time many of these kids get to the hospital, they have to be put temporarily on respirators because of depressed breathing." Disturbed by what they were seeing, Dr. O'Brien and her colleagues conducted a survey that year of 4,271 students from more than 10 universities in North Carolina. "We found that about a quarter of the kids who'd had a drink in the past 30 days said they were mixing alcohol with energy drinks, either the premixed kind or Red Bull and vodka. They got drunk twice as often and drank more per session than those who had alcohol without caffeine. They were much more likely to be injured, much more likely to be taken advantage of sexually or to take advantage of someone sexually, much more likely to drive drunk."

Colleges are on the front lines of this battle. Ramapo College in New Jersey banned energy drinks containing alcohol on campus in 2010 after a number of students were sent to the ER for alcohol-related reasons over a few weeks. James L. Gaudino, president of Central Washington University in Ellensburg, Wash., took similar action. "We banned alcoholic energy drinks when we became aware of the extraordinary threat they pose," he says. "What shocked us was the hospitalization of 11 students after a single party."

As outrage grew, the FDA [U.S. Food and Drug Administration] stepped in, and last year essentially ordered the makers of four brands, including Phusion Projects, which sells the cult favorite Four Loko, to remove the caffeine. Four Loko was reformulated and is now back on the market. The sweetened beverage no longer contains caffeine, but each 23.5-ounce can may have the alcohol equivalent of four to five beers. (Four standard beers for a female and five for a male over a two-hour period is considered binge drinking.) Though it's too early to tell if its popularity is abating, Four Loko, a.k.a. "Blackout in a Can," has been a hit on YouTube, with more than 5,000 videos extolling its virtues.

"Four Loko is everywhere," says Gabby K., 17, a high school junior in New Jersey. "It tastes like candy, so you can drink a lot of it fast. It's pretty potent and it only costs around $3 a can. It's a faster way to get drunk without having to deal with the taste of liquor." Gabby notes that the cans look a lot like iced tea. "It seems user-friendly," she says. But she won't drink it herself, pointing out that a number of kids in her school were hospitalized this year due to binge drinking. The makers of Four Loko reply: "We are fully committed to doing our part to ensure that our products are consumed legally and responsibly. Phusion Projects' marketing message is clear: If you are under the age of 21, respect the law and do not drink."

Even in its new incarnation, Four Loko falls into a category that teens love but that has authorities worried: flavored malt beverages. Like Four Loko, many of them are sold in brightly decorated 23.5-ounce cans and have an alcohol content of 12%.

On April 21, attorneys general from 16 states co-signed a letter to Pabst, makers of the malt beverage Blast. "We believe the manufacture and marketing of this flavored 'binge in a can' poses a grave public safety threat," the letter states. It cites concerns that Blast—with such varieties as strawberry lemonade and grape, a pervasive online presence, and the rap star Snoop Dogg as a spokesman—is aimed at underage drinkers. Jon Sayer, chief marketing officer of Pabst Brewing Company, issued this reply: "Blast is produced only for consumers above legal drinking age and is marketed as such." The president of Anheuser-Busch, meanwhile, announced in late May that the company will lower the alcohol content in its 24-ounce flavored malt beverage Tilt from 12% by volume to 8%.

There's a sense that you need to be wasted to go to a party, and if you're not, you won't have fun.

Drinking Games Go Hard-Core

Teens' growing preference for hard liquor over beer is also setting off alarms. Dr. Michael Siegel, professor at the Boston University School of Public Health, recently completed a study of high school students. "We found that, by far, liquor is the beverage of choice. This definitely represents a change."

Hard liquor is increasingly replacing beer in drinking games. "Kids easily drink seven or eight shots at a time," Gabby says of her buddies. But Dr. O'Brien notes, "That's low ballpark, from what we are seeing. Teens in our studies are having 10 or more drinks."

Helene F., 20, a junior in college in Colorado, explains the appeal: "Everyone's so much friendlier after a couple of drinks. It takes the pressure off. And if you want to get drunk quickly, shots are key. There's a sense that you need to be wasted to go to a party, and if you're not, you won't have fun. Certain events, like Halloween and homecoming, it's kind of guaranteed that kids are going to end up in hospitals." After 14 students were hospitalized during a graduation celebration in

2008, Colby College in Maine studied the issue and, in 2010, banned hard liquor on most of the campus.

"The adolescent brain is much more sensitive to alcohol toxicity than adults', including being vulnerable to cell death," says Dr. Fulton Crews, director of the Bowles Center for Alcohol Studies at the University of North Carolina School of Medicine. "Adolescents showed much more frontal cortical damage than adults. We found that one high dose of alcohol caused significant loss of brain stem cells."

Early drinking also poses a risk later in life. "If you start drinking early, you're 40% to 60% more likely to become an alcoholic, regardless of family history," Dr. Crews says. And studies indicate a potential for permanent memory impairment.

13

Drinking Alcohol While Pregnant Harms the Baby

March of Dimes

The March of Dimes, a nonprofit organization, was originally established by Franklin Delano Roosevelt to fight polio. Presently, the foundation's focus is on preventing birth defects, infant mortality, and premature birth.

Since no amount of alcohol use during pregnancy has been proven safe, women who are pregnant or trying to become pregnant should abstain from all forms of alcohol. Drinking alcohol during pregnancy greatly increases the risk of miscarriage, premature delivery, and the incidence of fetal alcohol spectrum disorders (FASD). It is estimated that every year in the United States as many as 40,000 babies are born with the effects of FASD, such as heart defects, mental retardation, stunted growth, psychiatric problems, and abnormal facial features.

Drinking alcohol during pregnancy can cause a wide range of physical and mental birth defects. The term "fetal alcohol spectrum disorders" (FASDs) is used to describe the many problems associated with exposure to alcohol before birth. Each year in the United States, up to 40,000 babies are born with FASDs.

Although many women are aware that heavy drinking during pregnancy can cause birth defects, many do not realize that moderate or even light drinking also may harm the fetus.

March of Dimes, "Alcohol and Drugs: Drinking Alcohol During Pregnancy," www.MarchofDimes.com, November 2008. Reproduced by permission.

In fact, no level of alcohol use during pregnancy has been proven safe. Therefore, the March of Dimes recommends that pregnant women do not drink any alcohol, including beer, wine, wine coolers and liquor, throughout their pregnancy and while nursing. In addition, because women often do not know they are pregnant for a few months, women who may be pregnant or those who are attempting to become pregnant should not drink alcohol.

Recent government surveys indicate that about 1 in 12 pregnant women drink during pregnancy. About 1 in 30 pregnant women report binge drinking (five or more drinks on any one occasion). Women who binge drink or drink heavily greatly increase the risk of alcohol-related damage to their babies.

The alcohol level of the baby's blood can be higher and remain elevated longer than the level in the mother's blood.

Hazards of Drinking Alcohol During Pregnancy

When a pregnant woman drinks, alcohol passes through the placenta to her fetus. In the fetus's immature body, alcohol is broken down much more slowly than in an adult's body. As a result, the alcohol level of the baby's blood can be higher and remain elevated longer than the level in the mother's blood. This sometimes causes the baby to suffer lifelong damage.

Drinking alcohol during pregnancy can cause FASDs, with effects that range from mild to severe. These effects include mental retardation; learning, emotional and behavioral problems; and defects involving the heart, face and other organs. The most severe of these effects is fetal alcohol syndrome (FAS), a combination of physical and mental birth defects.

Drinking alcohol during pregnancy increases the risk for miscarriage and premature birth (before 37 completed weeks of pregnancy). Studies also suggest that drinking during pregnancy may contribute to stillbirth. A 2008 Danish study found that women who binge drink three or more times during the first 16 weeks of pregnancy had a 56 percent greater risk for stillbirth than women who did not binge drink. Another 2008 study found that women who had five or more drinks a week were 70 percent more likely to have a stillborn baby than non-drinking women.

FAS is one of the most common known causes of mental retardation. It is the only cause that is entirely preventable. Studies by the Centers for Disease Control and Prevention (CDC) suggest that between 1,000 and 6,000 babies in the United States are born yearly with FAS.

Babies with FAS are abnormally small at birth and usually do not catch up on growth as they get older. They have characteristic facial features, including small eyes, a thin upper lip and smooth skin in place of the normal groove between the nose and upper lip. Their organs, especially the heart, may not form properly. Many babies with FAS also have a brain that is small and abnormally formed. Most have some degree of mental disability. Many have poor coordination, a short attention span and emotional and behavioral problems.

FAS is one of the most common known causes of mental retardation.

The effects of FAS and other FASDs last a lifetime. Even if not mentally retarded, adolescents and adults with FAS and other FASDs are at risk for psychological and behavioral problems and criminal behavior. They often find it difficult to keep a job and live independently.

Less Obvious Alcohol-Related Birth Defects

The CDC estimates that about three times the number of babies born with FAS are born with some, but not all, of the features of FAS. These FASDs are referred to as alcohol-related birth defects (ARBDs) and alcohol-related neurodevelopmental disorders (ARNDs).

- The term ARBDs describes physical birth defects that can occur in many organ systems, including the heart, liver, kidneys, eyes, ears and bones.

- The term ARNDs describes learning and behavioral problems associated with prenatal exposure to alcohol. These problems can include learning disabilities; difficulties with attention, memory and problem solving; speech and language delays; hyperactivity; psychological disorders and poor school performance.

Children with ARBDs and ARNDs do not have the characteristic facial features associated with FAS.

In general, ARBDs are more likely to result from drinking alcohol during the first trimester, when organs are forming rapidly. Drinking at any stage of pregnancy can affect the brain, resulting in ARNDs, and can also affect growth.

An older term called fetal alcohol effects (FAEs) is sometimes used to describe alcohol-related damage that is less severe than FAS. The more specific diagnostic categories of ARBDs and ARNDs are now more frequently used.

No level of drinking alcohol has been proven safe during pregnancy. According to the U.S. Surgeon General, the patterns of drinking that place a baby at greatest risk for FASDs are binge drinking and drinking seven or more drinks per week. However, FASDs can occur in babies of women who drink less.

Researchers are taking a closer look at the more subtle effects of moderate and light drinking during pregnancy.

- A 2002 study found that 14-year-old children whose mothers drank as little as one drink a week were significantly shorter and leaner and had a smaller head circumference (a possible indicator of brain size) than children of women who did not drink at all.

- A 2001 study found that 6- and 7-year-old children of mothers who had as little as one drink a week during pregnancy were more likely than children of non-drinkers to have behavior problems, such as aggressive and delinquent behaviors. These researchers found that children whose mothers drank any alcohol during pregnancy were more than three times as likely as unexposed children to demonstrate delinquent behaviors.

- A 2007 study suggested that female children of women who drank less than one drink a week were more likely to have behavioral and emotional problems at 4 and 8 years of age. The study also suggested similar effects in boys, but at higher levels of drinking.

- Other studies report behavioral and learning problems in children exposed to moderate drinking during pregnancy, including attention and memory problems, hyperactivity, impulsivity, poor social and communication skills, psychiatric problems (including mood disorders) and alcohol and drug use.

Because no amount of alcohol has been proven safe during pregnancy, a woman should stop drinking immediately if she even suspects she could be pregnant.

Questions Regarding the Effects of Alcohol

Is there a cure for FASDs? There is no cure for FASDs. However, a 2004 study found that early diagnosis (before 6 years of age) and being raised in a stable, nurturing environment can improve the long-term outlook for individuals with FASDs. Children who experienced these protective factors during their school years were two to four times more likely to avoid serious behavioral problems resulting in trouble with the law or confinement in a psychiatric institution.

If a pregnant woman has one or two drinks before she realizes she is pregnant, can it harm the baby? It is unlikely that the occasional drink a woman takes before she realizes she is pregnant will harm her baby. The baby's brain and other organs begin developing around the third week of pregnancy, however, and are vulnerable to damage in these early weeks. Because no amount of alcohol has been proven safe during pregnancy, a woman should stop drinking immediately if she even suspects she could be pregnant, and she should not drink alcohol if she is trying to become pregnant.

Is it safe to drink alcohol while breastfeeding? Small amounts of alcohol do get into breastmilk and are passed on to the baby. One study found that breastfed babies of women who had one or more drinks a day were a little slower in acquiring motor skills (such as crawling and walking) than babies who had not been exposed to alcohol. Large amounts of alcohol may interfere with ejection of milk from the breast.

For these reasons, the March of Dimes recommends that women not drink alcohol while they are breastfeeding. Similarly, the American Academy of Pediatrics (AAP) recommends that breastfeeding mothers not drink alcohol. However, according to the AAP, an occasional alcoholic drink probably doesn't hurt the baby, but a mother who has a drink should wait at least 2 hours before breastfeeding her baby.

Can heavy drinking by the father contribute to FASDs? There is no proof that heavy drinking by the father can cause FASDs. But men can help their partner avoid alcohol by not drinking during their partner's pregnancy. . . .

Because there currently is no way to predict which babies will be damaged by alcohol, the safest course is not to drink alcohol at all during pregnancy and to avoid heavy drinking during childbearing years (because about 50 percent of pregnancies are unplanned). All women who are considering becoming pregnant should stop drinking alcohol. Heavy drinkers should avoid pregnancy until they believe they can abstain from alcohol throughout pregnancy.

14

Alcohol Abuse Is Increasing Among Military Personnel

Robert A. Wascher

Robert A. Wascher, a physician and retired Army colonel, is the author of numerous papers, articles, columns, and book chapters on cancer and public health research findings. He is also a registered researcher with the National Institutes of Health.

Concerned about the physical and mental health of America's military personnel, the US Department of Defense funded a study to examine the incidence and severity of alcohol abuse both before and following deployment to combat zones. The study found that Reserve and National Guard soldiers deployed to combat zones had nearly twice the risk for binge drinking and other forms of alcohol abuse compared to non-deployed soldiers. If more is not done in the way of education, prevention, and treatment programs, a large-scale epidemic of alcoholism among military personnel and veterans will result.

War is, indeed, hell, and there is ample clinical data from every recorded conflict in human history confirming that increasing exposure to the horrors of war leads, inevitably, to increasing risks of subsequent mental illness and substance abuse. Certainly, the current and ongoing conflicts in Iraq and Afghanistan are, once again, confirming this particular adverse effect of war. Moreover, given the reduced manpower of the Active Duty armed services following the post-Cold War drawdown, the extensive and repeated deployment

Dr. Robert A. Wascher, "Alcohol Abuse Before & After Military Deployment," www.DoctorWascher.com, August 23, 2008. Reproduced by permission of the author.

of Reserve military forces and the "citizen-soldiers" of the National Guard has been a rather unique feature of the still smoldering conflict in Iraq, and the worsening tactical situation in the Afghanistan combat theater.

A Study of Alcohol Abuse in the Military

A new clinical research study, recently published in the [August 2008] *Journal of the American Medical Association*, reports on the incidence and severity of alcohol abuse among members of the armed forces both before and following deployment to combat zones since 2000. A notable feature of this clinical research study is that its authors are, themselves, members of several military and veterans' hospitals here in the United States.

The "Millennium Cohort Study," which is funded by the Department of Defense, is the largest long-term prospective healthcare study in military history, and currently includes nearly 150,000 participants. In this alcohol abuse sub-study, 48,481 participants completed confidential pre-deployment and post-deployment health questionnaires. Active Duty military members accounted for 26,613 of the participants, while the remaining 21,868 participants were members of the Reserve and National Guard forces. When broken down further, more than 5,000 of the study participants had been deployed to combat units, while a nearly equal number of participants had been deployed but were not exposed to combat operations. Finally, more than 37,000 of this study's participants were not deployed at all during the study.

Alcohol Abuse Increased Following Combat Service

Among the Reserve and National Guard troops who admitted to the consumption of alcohol prior to deploying into combat conditions, the prevalence of pre-deployment and post-deployment heavy weekly drinking was 9% and 13%, respectively, while the prevalence of binge-drinking was 53% and 53%, respectively, and the prevalence of social or legal problems related to alcohol use was 15% and 12%, respectively. More concerning were the Reserve and National Guard soldiers who deployed to combat units, and who indicated minimal alcohol use, or no alcohol intake at all, prior to being deployed. When these soldiers were again surveyed *after* their deployments, they reported a 9% prevalence of new-onset heavy weekly drinking, a 26% prevalence of new-onset binge-drinking, and a 7% prevalence of new-onset alcohol-related personal, social or legal problems. (The prevalence of new-onset alcohol abuse among Active Duty soldiers, following deployment to combat zones, was similar to that of their Reserve and National Guard brethren.)

The youngest soldiers were at the highest risk of newly engaging in these risky alcohol-related behaviors following combat deployments.

When the study's researchers further analyzed this self-reported data, they determined that the Reserve and National Guard soldiers who were deployed to combat zones had nearly twice the risk of becoming involved with new-onset heavy weekly drinking, binge-drinking, and alcohol-related troubles in their personal and professional lives when compared to their non-deployed fellow soldiers. Not surprisingly, the youngest soldiers were at the highest risk of newly engaging in these risky alcohol-related behaviors following combat deployments.

This study, which concentrated on the alcohol-related behaviors of Reserve and National Guard soldiers before and following combat zone deployments, found an alarming rise in new-onset alcohol abuse among this cohort of part-time military reservists and "citizen-soldiers," particularly among younger soldiers. Ultimately, with the exception of those who have paid the ultimate price, all of these deployed Active Duty, Reserve and National Guard soldiers will eventually return to civilian society and, based upon the results of this study, many of their lives will already have become ravaged by alcohol abuse, and other substance abuse, by the time they complete their military service. Chronic alcohol and drug abuse have long been known to be associated with an increased risk of divorce, unemployment, physical and mental illness, and criminal behavior. Unless more can be done to effectively (and preferably) preempt alcohol and substance abuse within the uniformed services, and to implement a more robust counseling and treatment program for military personnel and veterans who are already suffering from combat-related alcohol and substance abuse, our society is very likely now looking at the early phase of a large-scale epidemic of alcoholism and other substance abuse among the thousands of veterans who are returning from combat deployments, and who are returning to civilian life.

> *A national public health epidemic of combat-related alcohol and drug abuse is likely to follow in the aftermath of the two ongoing wars.*

The Veterans Administration, which is already reeling from its current burgeoning caseload of physically and psychologically wounded veterans from the ongoing wars in Iraq and Afghanistan, is unlikely to be able to cope adequately with the alcohol-related health and social problems of the many thousands of soldiers who are continuing to transition to civilian life. A national public health epidemic of combat-related alcohol and drug abuse is likely to follow in the aftermath of the two ongoing wars, much as was seen following the Vietnam War. Only a much greater emphasis on alcohol and drug abuse education, prevention and treatment within the uniformed services, and among our growing population of veterans from these two ongoing conflicts, is likely to reduce the scale of this growing epidemic, and which is, of course, one of the many terrible consequences of war.

Organizations to Contact

The editors have compiled the following list of organizations concerned with the issues debated in this book. The descriptions are derived from materials provided by the organizations. All have publications or information available for interested readers. The list was compiled on the date of publication of the present volume; the information provided here may change. Be aware that many organizations take several weeks or longer to respond to inquiries, so allow as much time as possible.

Al-Anon Family Groups

1600 Corporate Landing Parkway, Virginia Beach, VA 23454
(757) 563-1600 • fax: (757) 563-1655
e-mail: wso@al-anon.org
website: www.al-anon.alateen.org

Al-Anon is a fellowship of men, women, and children whose lives have been affected by an alcoholic family member or friend. Members share their experiences, strength, and hope to help each other and perhaps to aid in the recovery of the alcoholic. Al-Anon provides information on its local chapters and on its affiliated organization, Alateen. Its publications include the magazine *Al-Anon Faces Alcoholism 2011*, the monthly magazine the *Forum*, the semiannual *Al-Anon Speaks Out*, the bimonthly *Alateen Talk*, and several books, including *How Al-Anon Works*, *Paths to Recovery: Al-Anon's Steps, Traditions, and Concepts*, and *Discovering Choices*.

Alcohol Justice

24 Belvedere St., San Rafael, CA 94901
(415) 456-5692 • fax: (415) 456-0491
website: www.marininstitute.org

Alcohol Justice, formerly known as the Marin Institute, works to reduce alcohol problems by serving as an alcohol industry watchdog in order to advance public health and safety. Alcohol Justice promotes stricter regulation of the alcohol industry, stricter alcohol policies, higher taxes on alcoholic beverages, the removal of products aimed at young people from the market, restrictions on alcohol sales and promotionk, and greater state government controls over alcohol sales, in order to reduce alcohol-related problems. It publishes a blog, fact sheets, reports, and news alerts on alcohol policy, advertising, and other alcohol-related issues.

Alcoholics Anonymous (AA)

AA World Services, Inc., 475 Riverside Dr., 11th Floor
New York, NY   10115
(212) 870-3400 • fax: (212) 870-3003
website: www.aa.org

Alcoholics Anonymous is an international fellowship of people who are recovering from alcoholism. Because AA's primary goal is to help alcoholics remain sober, it does not sponsor research or engage in education about alcoholism. AA does publish a catalog of literature concerning the organization, the book *Alcoholics Anonymous: The Big Book*, as well as several pamphlets, including *Is A.A. for You?*, *This Is A.A.—An Introduction to the A.A. Recovery Program*, and *Frequently Asked Questions About AA*.

American Beverage Institute (ABI)

American Beverage Institute, 1090 Vermont Ave. NW, Ste. 800
Washington, DC   20005
(202) 463-7110
website: www.abionline.org

The American Beverage Institute is a restaurant industry trade organization that works to protect the consumption of alcoholic beverages in the restaurant setting. It unites the wine, beer, and spirits producers with distributors and on-premise retailers in this effort. ABI conducts research and education in an attempt to demonstrate that the vast majority of adults who drink alcohol outside of the home are responsible, law-abiding citizens. Its website includes fact sheets, press releases, and news articles on various issues, such as drunk-driving laws and checkpoint programs, and research reports including "There Are Thousands of Reasons Why We Should Do More to Stop Drunk Driving: The Case for Roving Patrols."

The Beer Institute
122 C St. NW, Ste. 350, Washington, DC   20001
(202) 737-2337 • fax: (202) 737-7004
e-mail: info@beerinstitute.org
website: www.beerinstitute.org

The Beer Institute is a trade organization that represents the beer industry before Congress, state legislatures, and public forums across the country. It sponsors educational programs to prevent underage drinking and drunk driving. On its website, the institute publishes press releases, studies, and reports, such as "Signs of Progress: Declines in Underage Drinking and Drunk Driving" as well as *Beer Institute Updates* and the *Beer Institute Newsletter.*

Center on Alcohol Marketing and Youth (CAMY)
Johns Hopkins Bloomberg School of Public Health, Suite 292
Baltimore, MD   21205
(410) 502-6579
e-mail: reck@camy.org
website: http://camy.org

Located at the Johns Hopkins Bloomberg School of Public Health, CAMY monitors the marketing practices of the alcohol industry in order to focus attention and action on industry practices that it asserts jeopardize the health and safety of America's youth. CAMY believes that reducing high rates of underage alcohol consumption and the suffering caused by alcohol-related injuries and deaths among young people requires using the public health strategies of limiting the access to and the appeal of alcohol to underage persons. Among CAMY's publications are the research reports *Youth Exposure to Alcohol Advertising on Television, 2001–2009* and *Youth Exposure to Alcohol Advertising in National Magazines 2001–2008,* the fact sheet *Alcohol Advertising and Promotion: Excerpts from The Surgeon General's Call to Action to Prevent and Reduce Underage Drinking,* and the press release *CAMY Statement on Action by the FDA to Issue Warnings to Manufacturers of Alcoholic Energy Drinks.*

Century Council

2345 Crystal Dr., Ste. 910, Arlington, VA   22202

(202) 637-0077 • fax: (202) 637-0079

website: www.centurycouncil.org

A nonprofit organization funded by America's liquor industry, the Century Council aims to fight drunk driving and underage drinking. It seeks to promote responsible decision-making about drinking and discourage all forms of irresponsible alcohol consumption through education, communication, research, law enforcement, and other programs. Its website offers fact sheets, press releases, and news articles on drunk driving, underage drinking, and other alcohol-related problems, as well as the report it co-sponsored "Communication Strategies for College Binge Drinking Prevention—The Students' Perspective."

Distilled Spirits Council of the United States (DISCUS)

1250 I St. NW, Ste. 400, Washington, DC   20005

(202) 628-3544

website: www.discus.org

The Distilled Spirits Council of the United States is the national trade association representing producers and marketers of distilled spirits in the United States. It seeks to ensure the responsible advertising and marketing of distilled spirits to adult consumers and to prevent such advertising and marketing from targeting individuals below the legal purchase age. DISCUS publishes fact sheets, news releases, and documents, including its "Code of Responsible Practices for Beverage Alcohol Advertising and Marketing" and "Distilled Spirits Industry Primer."

International Center for Alcohol Policies (ICAP)
1519 New Hampshire Ave. NW, Washington, DC 20036
(202) 986-1159 • fax: (202) 986-2080
e-mail: info@icap.org
website: www.icap.org

The International Center for Alcohol Policies is a nonprofit organization dedicated to helping reduce the abuse of alcohol worldwide and to promote understanding of the role of alcohol in society through dialogue and partnerships involving the beverage industry, the public health community, and others interested in alcohol policy. ICAP is supported by eleven major international beverage alcohol companies. ICAP publishes reports including "Alcohol and Violence: Exploring Patterns and Responses," and reviews, such as the "ICAP Periodic Review on Drinking and Culture."

Mothers Against Drunk Driving (MADD)
511 E. John Carpenter Freeway, Ste. 700, Irving, TX 75062
(877) 275-6233 • fax: (972) 869-2206/7
website: www.madd.org

MADD is a nonprofit organization that seeks to stop drunk driving, support those affected by drunk driving, prevent underage drinking, and promote stricter alcohol policy. MADD publishes the biannual interactive online magazine *MADDvocate* as well as a variety of fact sheets, brochures, and other materials on drunk driving.

National Center on Addiction and Substance Abuse (CASA) at Columbia University
633 Third Ave., 19th Fl., New York, NY 10017-6706
(212) 841-5200
Website: www.casacolumbia.org

CASA is a nonprofit organization affiliated with Columbia University. It works to educate the public about the problems of substance abuse and addiction and evaluate prevention, treatment, and law enforcement programs to address the problem. Its website contains op-ed articles on alcohol policy and the alcohol industry, the *CASAINSIDE* newsletter, and various reports, including "Adolescent Substance Use: America's #1 Public Health Problem."

National Council on Alcoholism and Drug Dependence (NCADD)

244 East 58th St., 4th Fl., New York, NY   10022

(212) 269-7797 • fax: (212) 269-7510

e-mail: national@ncadd.org

website: www.ncadd.org

NCADD is a volunteer health organization that helps individuals overcome addictions, advises the federal government on drug and alcohol policies, and develops substance abuse prevention and education programs for youth. It publishes press releases, news stories, fact sheets, including "Alcohol and Crime" and "Drinking and Driving," and self-tests, such as "Am I Alcoholic?"

National Institute on Alcohol Abuse and Alcoholism (NIAAA)

5635 Fishers Lane, MSC 9304, Betheseda, MD   20892

(301) 443-3860

website: www.niaaa.nih.gov

The National Institute on Alcohol Abuse and Alcoholism is one of the eighteen institutes that comprise the National Institutes of Health. NIAAA provides leadership in the national effort to reduce alcohol-related problems. NIAAA publishes the quarterly bulletin, *Alcohol Alert*; a quarterly scientific journal, *Alcohol Research and Health*; a newsletter that is published three times a year; and many pamphlets and brochures dealing with alcohol abuse and alcoholism. All of these publications, including NIAAA's congressional testimony, are available online.

Research Society on Alcoholism (RSA)
7801 N. Lamar Blvd., Ste. D-89, Austin, TX   78752-1038
(512) 454-0022 • fax: (512) 454-0812
e-mail: DebbyRSA@sbcglobal.net
website: www.rsoa.org

The RSA provides a forum for researchers who share common interests in alcoholism and provides testimony to Congress on alcohol research and related issues. The society's purpose is to promote research on the prevention and treatment of alcoholism and is working to increase the level of federal funding for alcohol research. It publishes the journal *Alcoholism: Clinical and Experimental Research* twelve times a year as well as the book series *Recent Advances in Alcoholism.*

Secular Organizations for Sobriety (SOS)
4773 Hollywood Blvd., Hollywood, CA   90027
(323) 666-4295 • fax: (323) 666-4271
e-mail: Sos@cfiwest.org
website: www.cfiwest.org/sos

SOS is a nonprofit network of groups dedicated to helping individuals achieve and maintain sobriety. The organization believes that alcoholics can best recover by rationally choosing to make sobriety rather than by making spirituality or religion a priority. Most members of SOS reject the spiritual basis of Alcoholics Anonymous and other similar self-help groups. SOS publishes the quarterly *SOS International Newsletter* and distributes the books *Unhooked: Staying Sober and Drug Free* and *How to Stay Sober: Recovery Without Religion,* written by SOS founder James Christopher.

Substance Abuse and Mental Health Services Administration (SAMHSA)
1 Choke Cherry Road, Rockville, MD   20857
(877) 726-4727 • fax: (240) 221-4292
e-mail: samhsainfo@samhsa.hhs.gov
website: www.samhsa.gov

SAMHSA is a division of the US Department of Health and Human Services that is responsible for improving the lives of those with or at risk for mental illness or substance addiction. SAMHSA provides the public with a wide variety of information on alcoholism and other addictions. Its publications include fact sheets, reports, news releases, and the bimonthly newsletter *SAMHSA News*. Publications in Spanish are also available.

Bibliography

Books

Kenneth Anderson
How to Change Your Drinking: A Harm Reduction Guide to Alcohol. 2nd Edition. New York: HAMS Harm Reduction Network, 2010.

Sarah Allen Benton
Understanding the High-Functioning Alcoholic: Professional Views and Personal Insights. Westport, CT: Praeger, 2009.

Allen Berger
12 Stupid Things that Mess Up Recovery: Avoiding Relapse Through Self-Awareness and Right Action. Center City, MN: Hazelden, 2008.

Rachael Brownell
Mommy Doesn't Drink Here Anymore: Getting Through the First Year of Sobriety. San Francisco: Conari Press, 2009.

Jason J. Burrow-Sanchez and Leanne S. Hawken
Helping Students Overcome Substance Abuse: Effective Practices for Prevention and Intervention. New York: Guilford Press, 2007.

Tian Dayton
Emotional Sobriety: From Relationship Trauma to Resilience and Balance. Deerfield Beach, FL: Health Communications, Inc., 2007.

George W. Dowdall
College Drinking: Reframing a Social Problem. Westport, CT: Praeger, 2009.

Jack H. Hedblom   *Last Call: Alcoholism and Recovery.* Baltimore: Johns Hopkins University Press, 2007.

Marya Hornbacher   *Sane: Mental Illness, Addiction, and the 12 Steps.* Center City, MN: Hazelden, 2010.

Barbara Joy   *Easy Does It, Mom: Parenting in Recovery.* San Francisco: Conari Press, 2009.

Merlene Miller and David Miller   *Staying Clean & Sober: Complementary and Natural Strategies for Healing the Addicted Brain.* Orem, UT: Woodland Publishing, 2005.

Cynthia Perkins   *Get Sober Stay Sober: The Truth About Alcoholism.* Yucca Valley, CA: Cynthia Perkins Publications & Consultations, 2009.

Richard S. Sandor   *Thinking Simply About Addiction: A Handbook for Recovery.* New York: Jeremy P. Tarcher/Penguin, 2009.

Jennifer Storm   *Blackout Girl: Growing Up and Drying Out in America.* Center City, MN: Hazelden, 2008.

Harold C. Urschel, III   *Healing the Addicted Brain: The Revolutionary, Science-Based Alcoholism and Addiction Recovery Program.* Naperville, IL: Sourcebooks, Inc., 2009.

| Kristina Wandzilak and Constance Curry | *The Lost Years: Surviving a Mother and Daughter's Worst Nightmare.* Santa Monica, CA: Jeffers Press, 2006. |

Periodicals and Internet Sources

| Lizette Alvarez | "After the Battle, Fighting the Bottle at Home," *New York Times*, July 8, 2008. |

| Sarah Allen Benton | "Mothers Can Be High-Functioning Alcoholics Too!," *Psychology Today*, October 20, 2009. |

| Ada Calhoun | "Moms Who Drink: No Joking After the Schuler Tragedy," *Time*, August 11, 2009. |

| Tracy Clark-Flory | "The Rise of Binge Drinking Women: Should We Blame Gender Equality or Booze Culture?," Salon.com, December 9, 2010. www.salon.com. |

| John Cloud | "Alcoholic Energy Drinks: A Risky Mix," *Time*, May 30, 2008. |

| Tian Dayton | "Diane Schuler: The Sad Legacy of Alcohol and Drug Abuse," *Huffington Post*, August 5, 2009. www.huffingtonpost.com. |

| Daniel J. DeNoon | "CDC: Binge Drinking 'Huge U.S. Health Problem,'" *WebMD*, October 5, 2010. www.webmd.com. |

Martin Downs   "Challenging Old Assumptions about
                      Alcoholism," *New York Times*,
                      February 9, 2011.

Larry   "Why Are Caffeinated Alcoholic
Greenemeier   Energy Drinks Dangerous?," *Scientific
                      American*, November 9, 2010.

Laura Hambleton   "Scientists Try to Assess the Impact
                      of Binge Drinking on the Brains of
                      Teens," *The Washington Post*,
                      December 6, 2010.

Robert J. Hawkins   "UCSD Researchers: No Amount of
                      Alcohol is Safe for Drivers," *San
                      Diego Union Tribune*, June 22, 2011.

Susan Donaldson   "Answer to Underage Drinking: Make
James   Legal," ABCNews.com, August 20,
                      2008.

Russ Juskalian   "The Kids Can't Help It," *Newsweek*,
                      December 16, 2010.

David Kesmodel   "Buzz Kill? Critics Target
                      Alcohol-Caffeine Drinks," *Wall Street
                      Journal*, August 3, 2009.

Sid Kirchheimer   "The Best Way to Reap Alcohol's
                      Health Benefits," *AARP Bulletin*,
                      December 21, 2010.

Deborah Kotz   "Women and Alcohol: How Much Is
                      Healthful?," *U.S.News & World
                      Report*, May 7, 2008.

Gretel C. Kovach   "Marines' Internal Foe: Alcohol
                      Abuse," *San Diego Union-Tribune*,
                      January 23, 2011.

Mayo Clinic   "Alcohol Use: If You Drink, Keep It Moderate," November 5, 2010. www.mayoclinic.com.

Michele Munz   "Youth Disrupted: Fetal Alcohol Symptoms Arise in Late Childhood and Elude Effective Treatment," *San Diego Union-Tribune*, November 23, 2010.

New York Times   "Should Parents Be Jailed When Kids Drink?," June 17, 2010.

Roni Caryn Rabin   "Alcohol's Good for You? Some Scientists Doubt It," *New York Times*, June 15, 2009.

Steven Reinberg   "Binge Drinking May Damage Teens' Brains," *U.S. News & World Report*, April 22, 2009.

Sally Satel and Scott Lilienfeld   "Medical Misnomer: Addiction Isn't a Brain Disease, Congress," Slate.com, July 25, 2007. www.slate.com.

ScienceDaily   "Teens Who Drink with Parents May Still Develop Alcohol Problems," January 27, 2010. www.sciencedaily.com.

Nancy Shute   "Early Alcohol Use Causes Big Problems, Even for 'Good Kids,'" *U.S.News & World Report*, October 20, 2008.

Molly Snyder   "Should Kids Sip Their Parents' Alcoholic Drinks?," OnMilwaukee.com, February 6, 2011. www.onmilwaukee.com.

Evan Thomas   "How to Fight Binge Drinking: Would Lowering the Legal Age Help Colleges Curb Alcohol Abuse?," *Newsweek*, September 10, 2008.

Michelle Trudeau   "Teen Drinking May Cause Irreversible Brain Damage," NPR.org, January 25, 2010.

John H. Tucker   "Fighting Binge Drinking on Campus? It Takes a Village," *Newsweek*, December 1, 2010.

Paul Von Zielbauer   "In Iraq, American Military Finds It Has an Alcohol Problem," *New York Times*, March 12, 2007.

Elizabeth Weise   "The Secret Lives of Female Alcoholics," *USA Today*, September 15, 2009.

Leah Zerbe   "Alcohol's Benefits Are Erased by Extra Drinking," *Rodale News*, February 18, 2010.

Gregg Zoroya   "Alcohol Abuse by GIs Soars Since '03," *USA Today*, June 19, 2009.

Index

A

J

Jellinek, E. M., 69
Journal of the American Medical Association, 120
Jungle Juice, 106

K

Kansas, 51

L

Liability laws, 7–9
Licensing system, 44–47
Lightner, Candy, 40
Liquor, hard, 110–111
Listfield, Emily, 105
Lopez, Adrian, 108

M

Manzardo, Ann M., 98
March of Dimes, 112, 113, 117
Media, 34
Mental retardation, 114
Military, 17, 48–49, 51, 55–56, 119–123
Millennium Cohort Study, 120–122
Miller, William, 103
Miscarriage, 114
Misconceptions. *See* Mythology and misconceptions
Moderation, 24–26, 28
Mothers Against Drunk Driving (MADD), 40
Mythology and misconceptions, 58–59, 73–74

N

National Guard personnel, 119–123
National Incident-Based Reporting System, 14–15
National Institute on Alcohol Abuse and Alcoholism, 11, 16, 59, 74
National Institute on Drug Abuse, 16
National Institutes of Health, 20, 21
National Minimum Drinking Age Act, 39–43, 51–52
National Study of Adolescent Drinking Behavior, 54
National Woman Abuse Prevention Project, 14
Neurology. *See* Brain science
New England Journal of Medicine, 20–21
Nurnberger, John, 73
Nursing mothers, 26

O

O'Brien, Mary Claire, 107, 108
Oxford Group, 95

P

Pabst Brewing Company, 110
Parental accountability, 7–8
Parties. *See* Drinking parties
Peer pressure, 33–34
Penalties in a graduated licensing system, 46–47
Penick, Elizabeth C., 98